The Din in
the Head

The Din in
the Head

E S S A Y S

Cynthia Ozick

HOUGHTON MIFFLIN COMPANY

BOSTON · NEW YORK

2006

Copyright © 2006 by Cynthia Ozick

All rights reserved

For information about permission to reproduce selections from
this book, write to Permissions, Houghton Mifflin Company,
215 Park Avenue South, New York, New York 10003.

Visit our Web site: www.houghtonmifflinbooks.com.

Library of Congress Cataloging-in-Publication Data

Ozick, Cynthia.
The din in the head : essays / Cynthia Ozick.
p. cm.
ISBN-13: 978-0-618-47050-1
ISBN-10: 0-618-47050-6
1. Literature, Modern — 20th century —
History and criticism.   I. Title.
PN771.O99 2006
809'.04— dc22
2005016102

NOTE: The essays on Helen Keller, Lionel Trilling,
and Gershom Scholem originally appeared in *The New Yorker*.

Illustrations © David Levine
Book design by Anne Chalmers
Typefaces: Janson Text, Deepdene, Type Embellishments

Printed in the United States of America

MP 10 9 8 7 6 5 4 3 2 1

For
Samuel and Rosie,
some day

ACKNOWLEDGMENTS

I am grateful for the kind attention of the literary editors who welcomed these essays in their first incarnations; and I am especially indebted to Henry Finder, Leon Wieseltier, and Anne Fadiman.

My thanks also to David Levine, whose ingenious drawings punctuate these pages.

Contents

The Din in
the Head

§ FOREWORD

ON DISCORD AND DESIRE

WHEN SUSAN SONTAG DIED in the winter of 2004 — at seventy-one, far too soon for her powers to have been exhausted or her intellect slaked — she left a memorable and mottled trail. Much of her life will endure in photographs — but cameras, she argued, do not so much defeat transience as render it "more acute." Still, here she is on the back cover of my browning paperback copy of *The Benefactor*, a first novel published in 1963, when she was thirty: dark-haired, dark-browed, sublimely perfected in her youth. The novel, which reads like an audacious, sly, somewhat stilted translation from the French of a nineteenth-century philosophical memoir, ends with "a photograph of myself" — the self of the old narrator, who is contemplating his death. How distant death must have seemed to the young novelist then! In another photograph, dated 1975, she is lying on her back, hands under her head, with strongly traced Picasso eyelids and serene lips less curled than Mona Lisa's: beautiful at forty-two. Like any celebrity, she could be watched as she aged. Ultimately there came the signature white slash through the blackened forelock, and the face grew not harder but hardier (despite recurrent illness, throughout which she was inordinately courageous). She had a habit of tossing back her long loose hair when it fell, as it did from moment to moment, over her eyes: the abrupt shake of the head, once girlish, turned incongruous in the sexagenarian. She was tall and big-shouldered. She dominated any room, any platform; her voice was pitched low, mannish, humorous, impassioned, impatient. She was more than a presence: it was as if she had been inscribed in a cartouche — a figure who had, in effect, founded the culture in which she moved. And wherever she moved, the currents flowed with her.

Only her politics could not be said to be mottled: it was all of a piece, early and late, standard-issue and stereotypical: you could find its like in any university or elitist periodical in the Western world. Her politics, to which she gave so much of her vitality, some of it bravely (in Sarajevo), some of it reflexively (almost everywhere else), was, I think, the least interesting because the most commonplace part of her, though it ran deep and she valued it: it contributed to her celebrity and sometimes to her notoriety. But her celebrity was not her fame. Her fame erupted out of the publication in *Partisan Review* of "Notes on Camp," the 1965 essay that brought her instant recognition, in which she defined taste as the paramount contemporary aesthetic principle. "Taste," she wrote, "governs every free — as opposed to rote — human response. Nothing is more decisive. There is taste in people, visual taste, taste in emotion — and there is taste in acts, taste in morality. Intelligence, as well, is a kind of taste: taste in ideas."

With this manifesto she nearly single-handedly (though she soon had an army behind her) altered the culture. "The best that has been thought and said"— Matthew Arnold's exalted old credo, long superannuated — devolved to "Whatever." If taste governs all, then distinctions melt away, and the jihadist's "taste in morality" is no worse than mine or yours, and choosing life or choosing death comes down to *chacun à son goût*.

But set all that aside: it counts as politics, so let it go. The culture of art is where Sontag left her indelible and individual mark; and fame is when the individual becomes the general. As she prophesied in *Against Interpretation*, published in 1964,

> All the conditions of modern life — its material plentitude, its sheer crowdedness — conjoin to dull our sensory faculties. And it is in the light of the condition of our senses, or capacities (rather than those of another age), that the task of a critic must be assessed. What is important now is to recover our senses. We must learn to *see* more, to *hear* more, to *feel* more.

This was less a summons to hedonism (though it was that too) than it was a denigration of history. The emphasis on "now," the quick dismissal of "another age," the repeated "our," the ardent call to *see, hear, feel,* meant that one would be open to seeing and hearing and feeling nearly everything that lay in one's path. It meant fusion rather than separation, it meant impatience with categories, it meant infinite appetite, it meant the end of the distinction between high and low. And the end of that distinction made a cut in the common understanding, so that Norman Mailer, for instance, could write of rampant subway graffiti by urban vandals as others had written of Bernini and Matisse. And oddly, oddly, oddly! — the newly elitist doctrine of "the condition of our senses" came to resemble the "I know what I like" of the once-upon-a-time philistines and Babbitts.

The cut has been made; there is no going back. Yet Sontag herself did, in her final years, long to go back. At a symposium only months before her death, condemning the prevalence of "the idea that anything is better than anything else," she announced what amounted to a catchall self-repudiation: "It is the triumph of a pernicious relativism. . . . I am certainly not prepared to say the satisfactions derived by art are no different structurally, in content, or in quality, or in importance, from other kinds of satisfactions. I am not prepared to think that the satisfaction that I might get in front of a Chardin, a Vermeer, or a Vuillard, is in any way similar to the satisfaction I would get watching a beautifully pitched baseball or inspecting a shoe collection." And she reflected in a late interview that she wished she had written novels instead of the essays that had overturned public sensibility: she had since reawakened to the seductions of the novel in its traditional realist dress. The two novels that were her last were light-years from her first — in tone, in structure, in aspiration. *The Benefactor* has no beneficiaries, no literary heirs, either in Sontag's own work or in that of her admirers. But society at large is heir to the cultural rupture, the linked discordances, that she championed.

In Eden, desire came before discord: first the apple, then the expulsion. In earthly life, discord will often precede desire, and chaos may wildly roil before the advent of clarity. In the period of Sontag's greatest influence, when she had declared realism in contemporary fiction to be passé, when novels were to be lauded for the aridness of a stringent metaphysics, a deep discord descended, a choking chaos suffocated. Or, I should say, this is what happened to me. Perhaps I was too easily swayed, or too readily impressed, or simply too timidly willing to accept what seemed at the time to be an enduring cultural authoritativeness. Or else a prior eternity, what until then had always been seen to be eternity, was now being crushed and thrown all over the horizon in irrelevant shards. That eternity was the belief, now grown useless, in the impermeability of high art; it was whatever principles of discrimination had been esteemed before. And what had been esteemed before was surely not "pop." All this was noted in the press in the elegiac reports of Sontag's death. For *The New Yorker*, Sontag was "a central figure in the aesthetic *bouleversement* of that period: the absorption of pop culture into high culture, the abandonment of classical form for modernist fracture, the enthronement of the shattered consciousness in place of realism and morals and beginning-middle-end." The *New York Times* remarked that Sontag — for all that "the life of the mind was for her something both rigorous and passionate"— could nevertheless link Patti Smith and Nietzsche. Under the old eternity, no one would dream of linking Patti Smith and Nietzsche. Under the new dispensation, the old eternity evaporated, differentiation was dust, high culture was porous and always open to Patti Smith.

I did not know who Patti Smith was; there was much afoot that I did not know as I sat in my room with its yellow wallpaper reading Henry James and volumes of Jewish history and *The Rise and Fall of the Roman Empire*. Yet here I was, all at once, steeped in discord and chaos: oh, the novel, the novel! Authority was demanding that I cease to trust its familiar form, that its familiar form was broken forever, and that to continue to hope for it in the old way was to be exiled to the writer's ultima Thule; only the marginal and the mediocre and the weak would fail to recognize this. Authority had wiped me out. And where was I, after all, and what was I, while Authority and its enviable sharers and minions were exulting in the great red-hot Downtown? In my room with the yellow wallpaper, writing, in defeat, a superannuated, superseded, and moribund novel that was already fouled by the stench of its predictable death throes.

So when, years later, Susan Sontag recanted — and who could claim that *The Volcano Lover* was *not* a recantation? — I was amazed by my own shallowness. And cowardice. And surrender of conviction. I had been taken in, I had allowed discord to rout desire, and here was Sontag herself, unembarrassed, undisgraced, rising out of calculated and self-made discord to claim the very desire the yellow wallpaper had been witness to: the old eternity: the novel in all its worn human fallible genuineness, unembellished by critical manifestos. As if a movie were being run in reverse: Adam and Eve propelled from east of Eden back into the verdant Garden.

It was the shock of Sontag's death, of having to speak her name in the past tense — she was the tone of the times, she was the muse of the age, she was one with her century, and look, her century, our century, the terrible twentieth, with all its blood and gas and gulags and crimsonly sordid Riefenstahl aesthetics, has gone into the past tense too — it was her death that pricked these reflections upon long-ago excesses. Excesses of critical pride, excesses of writers' vulnerability and demoralization: all of it vanished into nullity. My private war with Sontag can hardly count as a war if she had no inkling of the vanquished foot soldier in the yellow room. Yet she was victor only until irony itself won out — after all, she did recant! And it may not be mere sophistry to suggest that irony, and its sardonically grim grin, is the outcome of all wars, big and little. It is still possible, against the grain of Sontag's torn banner, to read Nietzsche — and Gibbon and Jewish history and George Eliot and E. M. Forster and Chekhov and so much else — without at the same time taking notice of Patti Smith.

And because there is no public punishment for it (except for the with-it ire of this or that hostile periodical), it is still possible to separate high from low, the enduring from the ephemeral; even to aver that intellect itself (and the ethical life as well) requires the making of distinctions — sorting out, acknowledging that one thing is not another thing, facing down blur and fusion and the moral and aesthetic confusion of false equivalence, and, in the name of appetite for life, false worth. Not for nothing does the Bible rule against yoking the heavy ox with the lightweight ass, a nuance that points to cultural seriousness: honor and especially justice to the earth's plenitude of differences. The ass does not have the force of the ox. And as the ironist Kafka knew, the hunger artist in pursuit of Less does not really practice a superior art.

I cannot say that all the essays in this book are unified by a single theme, though I suppose (like the ass straining to keep up with the ox) I could laboriously invent one for the occasion. On the other hand, most — not all — may be connected by what they are not, what they do not do. By and large, they do not celebrate trivia or hunger after the lesser — not, I hope, out of some monomaniacal purist arrogance to which they are not entitled, but because some matters are, in truth, more urgent, and significant, than others.

Or perhaps there *is* a unitary wave running through these pages: the notion of desire, ambition's womb; desire applied to the kind of willed (or dreamed) achievement that outlasts personality; that is the opposite of taste, which is all personality. Or call it by the plain and ultimately discordant name that Henry James, remembering the expulsion from bright-leafed Eden, gave to his own desire: *doubt*. "We do what we can — we give what we have. Our doubt is our passion and our passion is our task. The rest," he said, "is the madness of art." What reader, coming upon these reverberating words, whether for the first or the tenth or the hundredth time, will not take them to heart?

WHAT
HELEN KELLER
SAW

§ SUSPICION STALKS FAME; incredulity stalks great fame. At least three times — at ages eleven, twenty-three, and fifty-two — Helen Keller was assaulted by accusation, doubt, and overt disbelief. Though her luster had surpassed the stellar figures of generations, she was disparaged nearly as hotly as she was exalted. She was the butt of skeptics and the cynosure of idolators. Mark Twain compared her to Joan of Arc, and pronounced her "fellow to Caesar, Alexander, Napoleon, Homer, Shakespeare and the rest of the immortals." Her renown, he said, would endure a thousand years.

It has, so far, lasted more than a hundred, while steadily dimming. Fifty years ago, even twenty, nearly every ten-year-old knew who Helen Keller was. *The Story of My Life*, her youthful autobiography, was on the reading lists of most schools, and its author was popularly understood to be, if not the equal of Mark Twain's lavish exaggerations, a heroine of uncommon grace and courage, a sort of worldly saint. To admire her was an act of piety, and she herself, by virtue of the strenuous conquest of her limitations, was a living temple dedicated to the spirit of resurrection. Much of that worshipfulness has receded. Her name, if not entirely in eclipse, hardly elicits the awed recognition it once held.

No one nowadays, without intending satire, would place her alongside Caesar and Napoleon; and in an era of earnest disabilities legislation, with wheelchair ramps on every street corner, who would think to charge a stone-blind, stone-deaf woman with faking her experience?

Yet as a child she was accused of plagiarism, and in maturity of "verbalism," illicitly substituting parroted words for firsthand perception. All this came about because she was at once liberated by language and in bondage to it, in a way few other human beings, even the blind and the deaf, can fathom. The merely blind have the window of their ears, the merely deaf listen through their eyes. For Helen Keller there was no partially ameliorating "merely." What she suffered was a totality of exclusion. Her early life was meted out in hints and inferences — she could still touch, taste, smell, and feel vibrations; but these were the very capacities that turned her into a wild creature, a kind of flailing animal in human form.

The illness that annihilated Helen Keller's sight and hearing, and left her mute, has never been diagnosed. In 1882, when she was four months short of two years, medical knowledge could assert only "acute congestion of the stomach and brain," though later speculation proposes meningitis or scarlet fever. Whatever the cause, the consequence was ferocity — tantrums, kicking, rages — but also an invented system of sixty simple signs, intimations of intelligence. The child could mimic what she could neither see nor hear: putting on a hat before a mirror, her father reading a newspaper with his glasses on. She could fold laundry and pick out her own things. Such quiet times were few. Frenzied, tempestuous, she was an uncontrollable barbarian. Having discovered the use of a key, she shut up her mother in a closet. She overturned her baby sister's cradle. Her wants were concrete, physical, impatient, helpless, and nearly always belligerent.

She was born in Tuscumbia, Alabama, fifteen years after the Civil War, when Confederate consciousness and mores were still inflamed. Her father, who had fought at Vicksburg, called himself a "gentleman farmer," and edited a small Democratic weekly until, thanks to political influence, he was appointed a United States marshal. He was a zealous hunter who loved his guns and his dogs. Money was usually short; there were escalating marital angers. His second wife, Helen's mother, was younger by twenty years, a spirited woman of intellect condemned to farmhouse toil. She had a strong literary side (Edward Everett Hale, the New Englander who wrote "The Man Without a Country," was a relative) and read seriously and searchingly. In Charles Dickens's *American Notes* she learned about Laura Bridgman, a deaf-blind country girl who was being educated at the Perkins Institution for the Blind, in Boston. Her savior was its director, Samuel Gridley Howe, humanitarian activist and husband of Julia Ward Howe, author of "The Battle Hymn of the Republic": New England idealism at its collective zenith.

Laura Bridgman was thirteen years old when Dickens met her, and was even more circumscribed than Helen Keller — she could neither smell nor taste. She was confined, he said, "in a marble cell, impervious to any ray of light, or particle of sound." But Laura Bridgman's cell could be only partly unlocked. She never mastered language beyond a handful of words unidiomatically strung together. Scientists and psychologists studied her almost zoologically, and her meticulously intricate lacework was widely admired and sold. She lived out her entire life in her room at the Perkins Institution; an 1885 photograph shows her expertly threading a needle with her tongue. She too had been a normal child, until scarlet fever ravaged her senses at the age of two.

News of Laura Bridgman ignited hope — she had been socialized into a semblance of personhood, while Helen remained a small savage — and hope led, eventually, to Alexander Graham Bell. By then the invention of the telephone was well behind him, and he was tenaciously committed to teaching the deaf to speak intelligibly. His wife was deaf; his mother had been deaf. When the six-year-old Helen was brought to him, he took her on his lap and instantly calmed her by letting her feel the vibrations of his pocket watch as it struck the hour. Her responsiveness did not register in her face; he described it as "chillingly empty." But he judged her educable, and advised her father to apply to Michael Anagnos, Howe's successor as director of the Perkins Institution, for a teacher to be sent to Tuscumbia.

Anagnos chose Anne Mansfield Sullivan, a former student at Perkins. "Mansfield" was her own embellishment; it had the sound of gentility. If the fabricated name was intended to confer an elevated status, it was because Annie Sullivan, born into penury, had no status at all. At five she contracted trachoma, a disease of the eye. Three years on, her mother died of tuberculosis and was buried in potter's field — after which her father, a drunkard prone to beating his children, deserted the family. The half-blind Annie and her small brother Jimmie, who had a tubercular hip, were tossed into the poorhouse at Tewksbury, Massachusetts, among syphilitic prostitutes and madmen. Jimmie did not survive the appalling inhumanity of the place, and decades later, recalling its "strangeness, grotesqueness and even terribleness," Annie Sullivan wrote, "I doubt if life or for that matter eternity is long enough to erase the terrors and ugly blots scored upon my mind during those dismal years from 8 to 14." She never spoke of them, not even to her intimates.

She was rescued from Tewksbury by a committee investigating its spreading notoriety, and was mercifully transferred to Perkins. There she learned Braille and the manual alphabet and came to know Laura Bridgman. At the Massachusetts Eye and Ear Infirmary she underwent two operations, which enabled her to read almost normally, though the condition of her eyes continued fragile and inconsistent over her lifetime. After six years she graduated from Perkins as class valedictorian; Anagnos recognized in her clear traces of "uncommon powers." His affectionate concern was nearly a flirtation (he had once teasingly caressed her arm), while she, orphaned and alone, had made certain to catch his notice and his love. When her days at Perkins were ended, what was to become of her? How was she to earn a living? Someone suggested that she might wash dishes or peddle needlework. "Sewing and crocheting are inventions of the devil," she sneered. "I'd rather break stones on the king's highway than hem a handkerchief."

She went to Tuscumbia instead. She was twenty years old and had no experience suitable for what she would encounter in the despairs and chaotic defeats of the Keller household. She had attempted to prepare herself by studying Laura Bridgman's training as it was recorded in the Perkins archives. Apart from this, she had no resources other than the manual alphabet that enlivened her fingers, and the steely history of her own character. The tyrannical child she had come to educate threw cutlery, pinched, grabbed food off dinner plates, sent chairs tumbling, shrieked, struggled. She was strong, beautiful but for one protruding eye, unsmiling, painfully untamed: virtually her first act on meeting the new teacher was to knock out one of her front teeth. The afflictions of the marble cell had become inflictions. Annie demanded that Helen be separated from her family; her father could not bear to see his ruined little daughter disciplined. The teacher and her recalcitrant pupil retreated to a cottage on the grounds of the main house, where Annie was to be sole authority.

What happened then and afterward she chronicled in letter after letter, to Anagnos and, more confidingly, to Mrs. Sophia Hopkins, the Perkins housemother who had given her shelter during school vacations. Mark Twain saw in Annie Sullivan a *writer*: "How she stands out in her letters!" he exclaimed. "Her brilliancy, penetration, originality, wisdom, character and the fine literary competencies of her pen — they are all there." Her observations, both of herself and of the developing child, are kin, in their humanity, particularity, and psychological acumen, to philosophical essays. Jubilantly, and with preternatural awareness, she set down the progress, almost hour by hour, of Helen Keller's disentombment, an exuberant deliverance far more remarkable than Laura Bridgman's frail and inarticulate release. Howe had taught the names of things by attaching to them labels written in raised type — but labels on spoons are not the same as self-generated thoughts. Annie Sullivan's method, insofar as she recognized it formally as a method, was pure freedom. Like any writer, she wrote and wrote and wrote, all day long. She wrote words, phrases, sentences, lines of poetry, descriptions of animals, trees, flowers, weather, skies, clouds, concepts: whatever lay before her or came usefully to mind. She wrote not on paper with a pen, but with her fingers, spelling rapidly into the child's alert palm. Helen, quick to imitate yet uncomprehending, was under a spell of curiosity (the pun itself reveals the manual alphabet as magical tool). Her teacher spelled into her hand; she spelled the same letters back, mimicking unknowable configurations. But it was not until the connection was effected between finger-wriggling and its referent — the cognitive key, the insight, the crisis of discovery — that what we call mind broke free.

This was, of course, the fabled incident at the well pump, dramatized in film and (by now) collective memory, when Helen suddenly understood that the tactile pattern pecking at her hand was inescapably related to the gush of cold water spilling over it. "Somehow," the adult Helen Keller recollected, "the mystery of language was revealed to me." In the course of a single month, from Annie's arrival to her triumph in forcibly bridling the household despot, Helen had grown docile, eagerly willing, affectionate, and tirelessly intent on learning from moment to moment. Her intellect was fiercely engaged, and when language began to flood it, she rode on a salvational ark of words.

To Mrs. Hopkins Annie wrote ecstatically:

> Something within me tells me that I shall succeed beyond my wildest dreams. I know that [Helen] has remarkable powers, and I believe that I shall be able to develop and mould them. I cannot tell how I know these things. I had no idea a short time ago how to go to work; I was feeling about in the dark; but somehow I know now, and I know that I know. I cannot explain it; but when difficulties arise, I am not perplexed or doubtful. I know how to meet them; I seem to divine Helen's peculiar needs. . . .
>
> Already people are taking a deep interest in Helen. No one can see her without being impressed. She is no ordinary child, and people's interest in her education will be no ordinary interest. Therefore let us be exceedingly careful in what we say and write about her. . . . My beautiful Helen shall not be transformed into a prodigy if I can help it.

At this time Helen was not yet seven years old, and Annie was being paid twenty-five dollars a month.

The fanatical public scrutiny Helen Keller aroused far exceeded Annie's predictions. It was Michael Anagnos who first proclaimed her to be a miracle child — a young goddess. "History presents no case like hers," he exulted. "As soon as a slight crevice was opened in the outer wall of their twofold imprisonment, her mental faculties emerged full-armed from their living tomb as Pallas Athene from the head of Zeus." And again: "She is the queen of precocious and brilliant children, Emersonian in temper, most exquisitely organized, with intellectual sight of unsurpassed sharpness and infinite reach, a true daughter of Mnemosyne. It is no exaggeration to say that she is a personification of goodness and happiness." Annie, the teacher of a flesh-and-blood earthly child, protested: "His extravagant way of saying [these things] rubs me the wrong way. The simple facts would be so much more convincing!" But Anagnos's glorifications caught fire: one year after Annie had begun spelling into her hand, Helen Keller was celebrated in newspapers all over the world. When her dog was inadvertently shot, an avalanche of contributions poured in to replace it; unprompted, she directed that the money be set side for the care of an impoverished deaf-blind boy at Perkins. At eight she was taken to visit President Cleveland at the White House, and in Boston was introduced to many of the luminaries of the period: Oliver Wendell Holmes, John Greenleaf Whittier, Edward Everett Hale, and Phillips Brooks (who addressed her puzzlement over the nature of God). At nine, saluting him as "Dear Poet," she wrote to Whittier:

> I thought you would be glad to hear that your beautiful poems make me very happy. Yesterday I read "In School Days" and "My Playmate," and I enjoyed them greatly. . . . It is very pleasant to live here in our beautiful world. I cannot see the lovely things with my eyes, but my mind can see them all, and so I am joyful all the day long.

When I walk out in my garden I cannot see the beautiful flowers, but I know that they are all around me; for is not the air sweet with their fragrance? I know too that the tiny lily-bells are whispering pretty secrets to their companions else they would not look so happy. I love you very dearly, because you have taught me so many lovely things about flowers, birds, and people.

Her dependence on Annie for the assimilation of her immediate surroundings was nearly total—hands-on, as we would say, and literally so—but through the raised letters of Braille she could be altogether untethered: books coursed through her. In childhood she was captivated by *Little Lord Fauntleroy*, Frances Hodgson Burnett's story of a sunnily virtuous boy who melts a crusty old man's heart; it became a secret template of her own character as she hoped she might always manifest it—not sentimentally, but in full awareness of dread. She was not deaf to Caliban's wounded cry: "You taught me language, and my profit on't/ Is, I know how to curse." Helen Keller's profit was that she knew how to rejoice. In young adulthood, casting about for a faith bare of exclusiveness or harsh images, and given over to purifying idealism, she seized on Swedenborgian spiritualism. Annie had kept away from teaching any religion at all: she was a down-to-earth agnostic whom Tewksbury had cured of easy belief. When Helen's responsiveness to bitter social deprivation later took on a worldly strength, leading her to socialism, and even to unpopular Bolshevik sympathies, Annie would have no part of it, and worried that Helen had gone too far. Marx was not in Annie's canon. Homer, Virgil, Shakespeare, and Milton were: she had Helen reading *Paradise Lost* at twelve.

But Helen's formal schooling was widening beyond Annie's tutelage. With her teacher at her side, Helen spent a year at

Perkins, and then entered the Wright-Humason School in New York, a fashionable academy for deaf girls; she was its single deaf-blind pupil. She also pleaded to be taught to speak like other people, and worked at it determinedly—but apart from Annie and a few others who were accustomed to her efforts, she could not be readily understood. Speech, even if imperfect, was not her only ambition: she intended to go to college. To prepare, she enrolled in the Cambridge School for Young Ladies, where she studied mathematics, German, French, Latin, and Greek and Roman history. In 1900 she was admitted to Radcliffe (then an "annex" to Harvard), still with Annie in attendance. Despite her necessary presence in every class, diligently spelling the lecture into Helen's hand, and hourly wearing out her troubled eyes as she transcribed text after text into the manual alphabet, no one thought of granting Annie a degree along with Helen. It was not uncommon for Annie Sullivan to play second fiddle to Helen Keller; the radiant miracle outshone the driven miracle worker. Not so for Mark Twain: he saw them as two halves of the same marvel. "It took the pair of you to make a complete and perfect whole," he said. Not everyone agreed. Annie was sometimes charged with being Helen's jailer, or harrier, or ventriloquist. During examinations at Radcliffe, she was not permitted to be in the building. For the rest, Helen relied on her own extraordinary memory and on Annie's lightning fingers. Luckily, a second helper, adept at the manual alphabet, soon turned up: he was John Macy, a twenty-five-year-old English instructor at Harvard, a writer and editor, a fervent socialist, and, eventually, Annie Sullivan's husband, eleven years her junior.

The money for all this schooling, and for the sustenance of the two young women (both enjoyed fine clothes and vigorous horseback riding), came in spurts from a handful of very rich men

—among them John Spaulding, the Sugar King, and Henry Rogers, of Standard Oil. Helen charmed these wealthy eminences as she charmed everyone, while Annie more systematically cultivated their philanthropy. She herself was penniless, and the Kellers of Tuscumbia were financially useless. Shockingly, Helen's father had once threatened to put his little daughter on exhibit, in order to earn her keep. (Twenty years afterward, Helen took up his idea and went on the vaudeville circuit—she happily, Annie reluctantly—and even to Hollywood, where she starred in a silent movie, with the mythical Ulysses as her ectoplasmic boyfriend.)

At Radcliffe Helen became a writer. She also became a third party to Annie's difficult romance: whoever wanted Annie inevitably got Helen too. Drawn by twin literary passions like his own, Macy was more than willing, at least at first. Charles Townsend Copeland—Harvard's illustrious "Copey," a professor of rhetoric—had encouraged Helen (as she put it to him in a grateful letter) "to make my own observations and describe the experiences peculiarly my own. Henceforth I am resolved to be myself, to live my own life and write my own thoughts." Out of this came *The Story of My Life*, the autobiography of a twenty-one-year-old, published while she was still an undergraduate. It began as a series of sketches for the *Ladies' Home Journal*; the fee was three thousand dollars. John Macy described the laborious process:

> When she began work at her story, more than a year ago, she set up on the Braille machine about a hundred pages of what she called "material," consisting of detached episodes and notes put down as they came to her without definite order or coherent plan. Then came the task where one who has eyes to see must help her. Miss Sullivan and I read the discon-

nected passages, put them into chronological order, and counted the words to make sure the articles should be the right length. All this work we did with Miss Keller beside us, referring everything, especially matters of phrasing, to her for revision. . . .

Her memory of what she had written was astonishing. She remembered whole passages, some of which she had not seen for many weeks, and could tell, before Miss Sullivan had spelled into her hand a half-dozen words of the paragraph under discussion, where they belonged and what sentences were necessary to make the connection clear.

This method of collaboration, essentially mechanical, continued throughout Helen Keller's professional writing life; yet within these constraints the design, the sensibility, the cadences were her own. She was a self-conscious stylist. Macy remarked that she had the courage of her metaphors—he meant that she sometimes let them carry her away—and Helen herself worried that her prose could now and then seem "periwigged." To the contemporary ear, many of her phrases are too much immersed in Victorian lace and striving uplift—but the contemporary ear has no entitlement, simply by being contemporary, to set itself up as judge: every period is marked by a prevailing voice. Helen Keller's earnestness is a kind of piety; she peers through the lens of a sublimely aspiring poetry. It is as if Tennyson and the Transcendentalists had together got hold of her typewriter. At the same time, she is turbulently embroiled in the whole human enterprise—except, tellingly, for irony. She has no "edge," and why should she? Irony is a radar that seeks out the dark side; she had darkness enough. Her unfailing intuition was to go after the light. She flew toward it, as she herself said, in the hope of "clear and animated language." She knew what part of her mind was instinct and what part was information, and she was cautious about the difference; she was even suspicious, as she had good reason to be. "It is certain," she wrote, "that I cannot always distinguish my own thoughts from those I read, because what I read become the very substance and texture of my mind. . . . It seems to me that the great difficulty of writing is to make the language of the educated mind express our confused ideas, half feelings, half thoughts, where we are little more than bundles of instinctive tendencies." She, who had once been incarcerated in the id, did not require knowledge of Freud to instruct her in its inchoate presence.

The Story of My Life was first published in 1903, with Macy's ample introduction. He was able to write about Helen nearly as authoritatively as Annie, but also—in private—more skeptically: after his marriage to Annie, the three of them set up housekeeping in rural Wrentham, Massachusetts. Possibly not since the Brontës had so feverishly literary a crew lived under a single roof. Of this ultimately inharmonious trio, one, internationally famous for decades, was catapulted now into still greater renown by the recent appearance of her celebrated memoir. Macy, meanwhile, was discovering that he had married not a woman, a moody one at that, but the indispensable infrastructure of a public institution. As Helen's secondary amanuensis, he continued to be of use until the marriage collapsed. It foundered on his profligacy with money, on Annie's irritability—she fought him on his uncompromising socialism, which she disdained—and finally on his accelerating alcoholism.

Because Macy was known to have assisted Helen in the preparation of *The Story of My Life*, the insinuations of control that often assailed Annie now also landed on him. Helen's ideas, it was said, were really Macy's; he had transformed her into a

"Marxist propagandist." It was true that she sympathized with his political bent, but his views had not shaped hers. As she had come independently to Swedenborgian idealism, so had she come to societal utopianism. The charge of expropriation, of both thought and idiom, was old, and dogged her at intervals during much of her early and middle life: she was a fraud, a puppet, a plagiarist. She was false coin. She was "a living lie."

She was eleven when these words were first hurled at her, spewed out by a wrathful Anagnos. Not long before, he had spoken of Helen in celestial terms. Now he denounced her as a malignant thief. What brought on this defection was a little story she had written, called "The Frost King," which she sent him as a birthday present. In the voice of a highly literary children's narrative, it recounts how the "frost fairies" cause the season's turning.

> When the children saw the trees all aglow with brilliant colors they clapped their hands and shouted for joy, and immediately began to pick great bunches to take home. "The leaves are as lovely as flowers!" cried they, in their delight.

Anagnos—doubtless clapping his hands and shouting for joy —immediately began to publicize Helen's newest accomplishment. "The Frost King" appeared both in the Perkins alumni magazine and in another journal for the blind, which, following Anagnos, unhesitatingly named it "without parallel in the history of literature." But more than a parallel was at stake; the story was found to be nearly identical to "The Frost Fairies," by Margaret Canby, a writer of children's books. Anagnos was infuriated, and fled headlong from adulation and hyperbole to humiliation and enmity. Feeling personally betrayed and institutionally discredited, he arranged an inquisition for the terrified Helen, standing her alone in a room before a jury of eight Perkins officials and himself, all mercilessly cross-questioning her. Her mature recollection of Anagnos's "court of investigation" registers as pitiably as the ordeal itself:

> Mr. Anagnos, who loved me tenderly, thinking that he had been deceived, turned a deaf ear to pleadings of love and innocence. He believed, or at least suspected, that Miss Sullivan and I had deliberately stolen the bright thoughts of another and imposed them on him to win his admiration. . . . As I lay in my bed that night, I wept as I hope few children have wept. I felt so cold, I imagined that I should die before morning, and the thought comforted me. I think if this sorrow had come to me when I was older, it would have broken my spirit beyond repairing.

She was defended by Alexander Graham Bell, and by Mark Twain, who parodied the whole procedure with a thumping hurrah for plagiarism, and disgust for the egotism of "these solemn donkeys breaking a little child's heart with their ignorant damned rubbish! A gang of dull and hoary pirates piously setting themselves the task of disciplining and purifying a kitten that they think they've caught pilfering a chop!" Margaret Canby's tale had been spelled to Helen perhaps three years before, and lay dormant in her prodigiously retentive memory; she was entirely oblivious of reproducing phrases not her own. The scandal Anagnos had precipitated left a lasting bruise. But it was also the beginning of a psychological, even a metaphysical, clarification that Helen refined and ratified as she grew older, when similar, if more subtle, suspicions cropped up in the press, compelling her to interrogate the workings of her mind. *The Story of My Life* was attacked in the *Nation* not for plagiarism in the usual sense, but for the purloining of "things beyond her powers of perception with the assurance of one who has verified every word. . . . One resents the pages of second-hand description of natural objects." The reviewer blamed her for the sin of vicariousness: "all her knowledge," he insisted, "is hearsay knowledge."

It was almost a reprise of the Perkins tribunal: she was again being confronted with the charge of inauthenticity. Anagnos's rebuke—"Helen Keller is a living lie"—regularly resurfaced, sometimes less harshly, sometimes as acerbically, in the form of a neurologist's or a psychologist's assessment, or in the reservations of reviewers. A French professor of literature, who was himself blind, determined that she was "a dupe of words, and her aesthetic enjoyment of most of the arts is a matter of auto-suggestion rather than perception." A *New Yorker* interviewer complained, "She talks bookishly. . . . To express her ideas, she falls back on the phrases she has learned from books, and uses words that sound stilted, poetical metaphors." A professor of neurology at Columbia University, after a series of tests, pooh-poohed the claim that her remaining senses might be in any way extraordinary—the acuity of her touch and smell, he concluded, was no different from that of other mortals. "That's a stab at my vanity," she joked.

But the cruelest appraisal of all came, in 1933, from Thomas Cutsforth, a blind psychologist. By this time Helen was fifty-three, and had published four additional autobiographical volumes. Cutsforth disparaged everything she had become. The wordless child she once was, he maintained, was closer to reality than what her teacher had made of her through the imposition of "word-mindedness." He objected to her use of images such as "a mist of green," "blue pools of dog violets," "soft clouds tumbling." All that, he protested, was "implied chicanery" and "a birthright sold for a mess of verbiage." He criticized the aims of the educational system in which she has been confined during her whole life. Literary expression has been the goal of her formal education. Fine writing, regardless of its meaningful content, has been the end toward which both she and her teacher have striven. . . . Her own experiential life was rapidly made secondary, and it was regarded as such by the victim. . . . Her teacher's ideals became her ideals, her teacher's likes became her likes, and whatever emotional activity her teacher experienced she experienced.

For Cutsforth—and not only for him—Helen Keller was the victim of language rather than its victorious master. She was no better than a copy; whatever was primary, and thereby genuine, had been stamped out. As for Annie, while here she was pilloried as the callous instrument of her pupil's victimization, elsewhere she was pitied as a woman cheated of her own life by having sacrificed it to serve another. Either Helen was Annie's slave, or Annie was Helen's.

Once again Helen had her faithful defenders. The philosopher Ernst Cassirer reflected that "a human being in the construction of his human world is not dependent upon the quality of his sense material." Even more trenchantly, a *New York Times* editor quoted Cicero: "When Democritus lost his sight he could not, to be sure, distinguish black from white; but all the same he could distinguish good from bad, just from unjust, honorable from disgraceful, expedient from inexpedient, great from small, and it was permitted him to live happily without seeing changes of color; it was not permissible to do so without true ideas."

But Helen did not depend on philosophers, ancient or modern, to make her case. She spoke for herself: she was nobody's puppet, her mind was her own, and she knew what she saw. Once, having been taken to the uppermost viewing platform of what was then the tallest building in the world, she defined her condition:

> I will concede that my guides saw a thousand things that escaped me from the top of the Empire State Building, but I am not envious. For imagination creates distances that reach to the end of the world. . . . There was the Hudson—more like the flash of a swordblade than a noble river. The little island of Manhattan, set like a jewel in its nest of rainbow waters, stared up into my face, and the solar system circled about my head!

Her rebuttal to word-mindedness, to vicariousness, to implied chicanery and the living lie, was inscribed deliberately and defiantly in her daring images of swordblade and rainbow waters. That they were derived was no reason for her to be deprived—why should she alone be starved of enchantment? The deaf-blind person, she wrote, "seizes every word of sight and hearing, because his sensations compel it. Light and color, of which he has no tactual evidence, he studies fearlessly, believing that all humanly knowable truth is open to him." She was not ashamed of talking bookishly: it meant a ready access to the storehouse of history and literature. She disposed of her critics with a dazzling apothegm: "The bulk of the world's knowledge is an imaginary construction," and went on to contend that history itself "is but a mode of imagining, of making us see civilizations that no longer appear upon the earth." Those who ridiculed her rapturous rendering of color she dismissed as "spirit-vandals" who would force her "to bite the dust of material things." Her idea of the subjective onlooker was broader than that of physics, and while "red" may denote an explicit and measurable wavelength in the visible spectrum, in the mind it is flittingly fickle (and not only for the blind), varying from the bluster of rage to the reticence of a blush: physics cannot cage metaphor.

She saw, then, what she wished, or was blessed, to see, and rightly named it imagination. In this she belongs to a wider class than that narrow order of the tragically deaf-blind. Her class, her tribe, hears what no healthy ear can catch, and sees what no eye chart can quantify. Her common language was not with the man who crushed a child for memorizing what the fairies do, or with the carpers who scolded her for the crime of a literary vocabulary. She was a member of the race of poets, the Romantic kind; she was close cousin to those novelists who write not only what they do not know, but what they cannot possibly know.

And though she was early taken in hand by a writerly intelligence leading her purposefully to literature, it was hardly in the power of the manual alphabet to pry out a writer who was not already there. Laura Bridgman stuck to her lace making, and with all her senses intact might have remained a needlewoman. John Macy believed finally that between Helen and Annie there was only one genius—his wife. Helen's intellect, he asserted, was "stout and energetic, of solid endurance," able to achieve through patience and toil, but void of real brilliance. In the absence of Annie's inventiveness and direction, he implied, Helen's efforts would show up as the lesser gifts they were. This did not happen. Annie died, at seventy, in 1936, four years after Macy; they had long been estranged. By then her always endangered eyesight had deteriorated; depressed, obese, cranky, and inconsolable, she had herself gone blind. Helen came under the care of her secretary, Polly Thomson, a Scotswoman who was both possessively loyal and dryly unliterary: the scenes she spelled into Helen's hand never matched Annie's quicksilver evocations.

But even as she mourned the loss of her teacher, Helen

flourished. Annie was dead; only the near-at-hand are indispensable. With the assistance of Nella Henney, Annie Sullivan's biographer, she continued to publish journals and memoirs. She undertook grueling visits to Japan, India, Israel, Europe, Australia, everywhere championing the blind, the deaf, the dispossessed. She was indefatigable until her very last years, and died in 1968 weeks before her eighty-eighth birthday.

Yet the story of her life is not the good she did, the panegyrics she inspired, or the disputes (genuine or counterfeit? victim or victimizer?) that stormed around her. The most persuasive story of Helen Keller's life is what she said it was: "I observe, I feel, I think, I imagine."

She was an artist. She imagined.

"Blindness has no limiting effect on mental vision. My intellectual horizon is infinitely wide," she was impelled to argue again and again. "The universe it encircles is immeasurable." And like any writer making imagination's mysterious claims before the material-minded, she had cause enough to cry out, "Oh, the supercilious doubters!"

But it was not herself alone she was shielding from these skirmishes: she was a warrior in a wide and thorny conflict. Helen Keller, if we are presumptuous enough to reduce her so, can be taken to be a laboratory for empirical demonstration. Do we know only what we see, or do we see what we somehow already know? Are we more than the sum of our senses? Does a picture — whatever strikes the retina — engender thought, or does thought create the picture? Can there be subjectivity without an object to glance off from? Metaphysicians and other theorists have their differing notions, to which the ungraspable organism that is Helen Keller is a retort. She is not an advocate for one side or the other in the ancient debate concerning the nature of the real. She is not a philosophical or neurological or therapeutic topic. She stands for enigma, and against obtuseness; there lurks in her still the angry child who demanded to be understood, yet could not be deciphered. She refutes those who cannot perceive, or do not care to value, what is hidden from sensation.

Against whom does she rage, whom does she refute? The mockers of her generation and ours. The psychiatrist Bruno Bettelheim, for instance. "By pretending to have a full life," he warned in a 1990 essay, "by pretending that through touch she knew what a piece of sculpture, what flowers, what trees were like, that through the words of others she knew what the sky or clouds looked like, by pretending that she could hear music by feeling the vibrations of musical instruments," she fooled the world into thinking the "terribly handicapped are not suffering deeply every moment of their lives." Pretender, trickster: this is what the notion of therapy makes of "the words of others," which we more commonly term experience; heritage; literature. At best the therapist pities, at worst he sees delusion. Perhaps Helen Keller did suffer deeply. Then all the more honor to the flashing embossments of the artist's mask. Oddly, practitioners of psychology—whom one would least expect to be literalists—have been quickest to blame her for imposture. Let them blame Keats, too, for his delusionary "Heard melodies are sweet, but those unheard are sweeter," and for his phantom theme of negative capability, the poet's oarless casting about for the hallucinatory shadows of desire.

Helen Keller's lot, it turns out, was not unique. "We work in the dark," Henry James affirmed, on behalf of his own art, and so did she. It was the same dark. She knew her Wordsworth: "Visionary power/Attends the motions of the viewless winds/Embodied in the mystery of word:/There, darkness makes abode."

She fought the debunkers who, for the sake of a spurious honesty, would denude her of landscape and return her to the marble cell. She fought the iron pragmatists who meant to disinherit her, and everyone, of poetry. She fought the tin ears who took imagining to be mendacity. Her legacy, after all, is an epistemological marker of sorts: proof of the real existence of the mind's eye.

In one respect, though, she was incontrovertibly as fraudulent as the cynics charged. She had always been photographed in profile: this hid her disfigured left eye. In maturity she had both eyes surgically removed and replaced with glass—an expedient known only to those closest to her. Everywhere she went, her sparkling blue prosthetic eyes were admired for their living beauty and humane depth.

Young Tolstoy:
An Apostle of Desire

§ CONTEMPLATING THE UNPREDICTABLE trajectory of Tolstoy's life puts one in mind of those quizzical Max Beerbohm caricatures, wherein an old writer confronts—with perplexity, if not with contempt—his young self. So here is Tolstoy at seventy-two, dressed like a *muzhik* in belted peasant tunic and rough peasant boots, with the long hoary priestly beard of a vagabond pilgrim, traveling third class on a wooden bench in a fetid train carriage crowded with the ragged poor. In the name of the equality of souls he has turned himself into a cobbler; in the name of the pristine Jesus he is estranged from the rites and beliefs of Russian Orthodoxy; in the name of Christian purity he has abandoned wife and family. He is ascetic, celibate, pacifist. To the multitude of his followers and disciples (Gandhi among them), he is a living saint.

And over here—in the opposite panel—is Tolstoy at twenty-three: a dandy, a horseman, a soldier, a hunter, a tippler, a gambler, a wastrel, a frequenter of fashionable balls, a carouser among gypsies, a seducer of servant girls; an aristocrat immeasurably wealthy, inheritor of a far-flung estate, master of hundreds of serfs. Merely to settle a debt at cards, he thinks nothing of selling (together with livestock and a parcel of land) several scores of serfs.

In caricature the two—the old Tolstoy, the young Tolstoy—cannot be reconciled. In conscience, in contriteness, they very nearly can. The young Tolstoy's diaries are self-interrogations that lead to merciless self-indictments, pledges of spiritual regeneration, and utopian programs for both personal renewal and the amelioration of society at large. But the youthful reformer is also a consistent backslider. At twenty-six he writes scathingly, "I am ugly, awkward, untidy and socially uncouth. I am irritable and tiresome to others; immodest, intolerant and shy as a child. In other words, a boor. . . . I am excessive, vacillating, unstable, stupidly vain and aggressive, like all weaklings. I am not courageous. I am so lazy that idleness has become an ineradicable habit with me." After admitting nevertheless to a love of virtue, he confesses: "Yet there is one thing I love more than virtue: fame. I am so ambitious, and this craving in me has had so little satisfaction, that if I had to choose between fame and virtue, I am afraid I would very often opt for the former."

A year later, as an officer stationed at Sevastopol during the Crimean War, he is all at once struck by a "grandiose, stupendous" thought. "I feel capable of devoting my life to it. It is the founding of a new religion, suited to the present state of mankind: the religion of Christ, but divested of faith and mysteries, a practical religion, not promising eternal bliss but providing bliss here on earth. I realize," he acknowledges, "that this idea can only become a reality after several generations have worked consciously toward it," but in the meantime he is still gambling, losing heavily, and complaining of "fits of lust" and "criminal sloth." The idealist is struggling in the body of the libertine; and the libertine is always, at least in the diaries, in pursuit of self-cleansing.

It was in one of these recurrent moods of purification in the wake of relapse that Tolstoy determined, in 1851, to go to the

Caucasus, an untamed region of mountains, rivers, and steppes. He had deserted his university studies; he was obsessed by cards, sex, illusory infatuation; he was footloose and parentless. His mother had died when he was two, his father seven years later. He had been indulged by adoring elderly aunts, patient tutors, obsequious servants (whom he sometimes had flogged). When the family lands fell to him, he attempted to lighten the bruised and toilsome lives of his serfs; the new threshing machine he ordered failed, and behind his back they called him a madman. Futility and dissatisfaction dogged him. Once more a catharsis was called for, the hope of a fresh start innocent of salons and balls, in surroundings unspoiled by fashion and indolence, far from the silks and artifice of Moscow and St. Petersburg. Not fragile vows in a diary, but an act of radical displacement. If Rousseau was Tolstoy's inspiration—the philosopher's dream of untutored nature—his brother Nicholas, five years his senior, was his opportunity. Nicholas was an officer at a *stanitsa*, a Cossack outpost, in the Caucasus. Tolstoy joined him there as a zealous cadet. The zeal was for the expectation of military honors, but even more for the exhilaration of seeing Cossack life up close. The Cossacks, like their untrammeled landscape, were known to be wild and free; they stood for the purity of natural man, untainted by the affectations of an overrefined society.

So thinks Olenin, the young aristocrat whose sensibility is the motivating fulcrum of *The Cossacks*, the novel Tolstoy began in 1852, shortly after his arrival in the Caucasus. Like Tolstoy himself, Olenin at eighteen

> had been free as only the rich, parentless young of Russia's eighteen-forties could be. He had neither moral nor physical fetters. He could do anything he wanted. . . . He gave himself

up to all his passions, but only to the extent that they did not bind him. . . . Now that he was leaving Moscow he was in that happy, youthful state of mind in which a young man, thinking of the mistakes he has committed, suddenly sees things in a different light—sees that these past mistakes were incidental and unimportant, that back then he had not wanted to live a good life, but that now, as he was leaving Moscow, a new life was beginning in which there would be no mistakes and no need for remorse. A life in which there would be nothing but happiness.

But the fictional Olenin is Tolstoy's alter ego only in part. After months of dissipation, each comes to the Caucasus as a volunteer soldier attached to a Russian brigade; each is in search of clarity of heart. Olenin, though, is a wistful outsider who is gradually drawn into the local mores, while his creator is a sophisticated and psychologically omniscient sympathizer with the eye of an evolving anthropologist.

After starting work on *The Cossacks*, Tolstoy soon set it aside and did not return to finish it until an entire decade had elapsed. In the interval, he continued to serve in the military for another three years; he published stories and novels; he traveled in Europe; he married. Still, there is little evidence of a hiatus; the narrative of *The Cossacks* is nearly seamless. It pauses only once, of necessity, in chapter four—which, strikingly distanced from character and story, and aiming to explain Cossack culture to the uninitiated, reads much like an entry in a popular encyclopedia. Terrain and villages are minutely noted; also dress, weapons, songs, shops, vineyards, hunting and fishing customs, the status and behavior of girls and women. "At the core of [Cossack] character," Tolstoy writes, "lies love of freedom, idleness, plunder, and war. . . . A Cossack bears less hatred for a Chechen warrior who has killed his brother than for a Russian soldier billeted with him. . . . A dashing young Cossack will flaunt his knowledge of Tatar, and will even speak it with his brother Cossacks when he drinks and carouses with them. And yet this small group of Christians, cast off on a distant corner of the earth, surrounded by Russian soldiers and half-savage Mohammedan tribes, regard themselves as superior, and acknowledge only other Cossacks as their equals." On and on, passage after descriptive passage, these living sketches of Cossack society accumulate—so much so, that a contemporary critic observed, "A score of ethnological articles could not give a more complete, exact, and colorful picture of this part of our land."

The name "Cossack" appears to derive from a Turkic root meaning freebooter, or, in a milder interpretation, adventurer. As a distinct population group, the Cossacks grew out of a movement of peasants escaping serfdom, who in the fifteenth century fled to the rivers and barren plains of Ukraine and southeastern Russia, seeking political autonomy. Having established self-governing units in areas close to Muslim-dominated communities, whose dress and outlook they often assimilated, the Cossacks were eventually integrated into the Russian military; their villages became army outposts defending Russia against the furies of neighboring Chechen fighters. It is into this history—that of an admirable, courageous, independent people, in gaudy Circassian costume, the women as splendidly self-reliant as the men—that Tolstoy sets Olenin, his citified patrician. And it is vital for Tolstoy to halt his story before it has barely begun—momentarily to obliterate it from view—in order to supply his readers in Moscow and St. Petersburg with a geographical and sociological portrait of the land Olenin is about to encounter. For such readers, as for Olenin, the Cossacks are meant to carry the romantic magnetism of the noble primitive.

But there is a different, and far more sinister, strain of Cossack history, which Tolstoy omits, and which later readers—we who have passed through the bloody portals of the twentieth century—cannot evade. Tolstoy saw, and survived, war. We too have seen war; but we have also seen, and multitudes have not survived, genocide. The most savage of wars boasts a cause, or at least a pretext; genocide pretends nothing other than the lust for causeless slaughter. And it is genocide, it must be admitted, that is the ineluctable resonance of the term "Cossacks." Writing one hundred and fifty years ago, Tolstoy registers no consciousness of this genocidal association—the long trail of Cossack pogroms and butcheries; hence the Cossacks of his tale are merely conventional warriors. Lukashka, a young fighter, coldly fells a Chechen enemy; his companions vie for possession of the dead man's coat and weapons. Afterward they celebrate with pails of vodka. A flicker of humane recognition touches the killer, but is quickly snuffed: "'He too was a man,' Lukashka said, evidently admiring the dead Chechen." To which a fellow Cossack replies, "Yes, but if it had been up to him, he wouldn't have shown *you* any mercy." It is the language of war, of warriors, heinous enough, and regrettable—still, nothing beyond the commonplace.

Then is it conceivable that we know more, or wish to know more, than the majestic Tolstoy? Along with Shakespeare and Dante, he stands at the crest of world literature: who can own a deeper sensibility than that of Tolstoy, who can know more than he? But we do know more: through the grimness of time and the merciless retina of film, we have been witness to indelible scenes of genocide. And it is because of this ineradicable contemporary knowledge of systematic carnage that Cossack history must now, willy-nilly, trigger tremor and alarm. Fast-forward from Tolstoy's 1850s to the year 1920: Isaac Babel, a Soviet reporter, is riding with the Red Cossacks (a brigade that has made common cause with the Bolsheviks); they are hoping forcibly to bring Poland to Communism. Babel, like Olenin, is a newcomer to the ways of the Cossacks, and he too is entranced by nature's stalwarts. In his private diary he marvels at these skilled and fearless horsemen astride their thundering mounts: "inexplicable beauty," he writes, "an awesome force advancing . . . red flags, a powerful, well-knit body of men, confident commanders, calm and experienced eyes." And again, describing a nocturnal tableau: "They eat together, sleep together, a splendid silent companionship . . . they sing songs that sound like church music in lusty voices, their devotion to horses, beside each man a little heap—saddle, bridle, ornamental saber, greatcoat."

But there is a lethal underside to this muscular idyll. Daily the Cossacks storm into the little Jewish towns of Polish Galicia, looting, burning, torturing, raping, branding, desecrating, murdering: they are out to slaughter every living Jew. Babel, a Jew who will become one of Russia's most renowned writers (and whom the Soviet secret police will finally execute), conceals his identity: no Jew can survive when Cossacks are near. (My own mother, who emigrated from czarist Russia in 1906 at the age of nine, once confided, in a horrified whisper, how a great-uncle, seized in a Cossack raid, was tied by his feet to the tail of a horse; the Cossack galloped off, and the man's head went pounding on cobblestones until the skull was shattered.)

Tolstoy did not live to see the atrocities of 1920; he died in 1910, and by then he had long been a Christian pacifist; but surely he was aware of other such crimes. The Cossack depredations of the nineteenth century are infamous; yet these, and the mass killings Babel recorded, hardly weigh at all in comparison with the Chmielnicki massacres that are the bloodiest blot on

Cossack history. In a single year, between 1648 and 1649, under the leadership of Bogdan Chmielnicki, Cossacks murdered three hundred thousand Jews, a number not exceeded until the rise of the genocidal Nazi regime.

None of this, it goes without saying, forms the background of Tolstoy's novel; *The Cossacks*, after all, is a kind of love story: its theme is longing. The seventeenth century is buried beyond our reach, and already the events of the middle of the twentieth have begun to recede into forgetfulness. All the same, the syllables of "Cossacks" even now retain their fearful death toll, and a reader of our generation who is not historically naïve, or willfully amnesiac, will not be deaf to their sound.

Yet Tolstoy's stories are above all always humane, and his depiction of his Cossacks is vigorously individuated and in many ways unexpectedly familiar. They are neither glorified nor demeaned, and they are scarcely the monsters of their collective annals; if they are idiosyncratic, it is only in the sense of the ordinary human article. *The Cossacks* was immediately acclaimed. Turgenev, older than Tolstoy by ten years, wrote rapturously, "I was carried away." Turgenev's colleague, the poet Afanasy Fet, exclaimed, "The ineffable superiority of genius!" and declared *The Cossacks* to be a masterpiece; and so it remains, validated by permanence. Then what are we to do with what we know? How are we to regard Tolstoy, who, though steeped in principles of compassion, turned away from what *he* knew?

The answer, I believe, lies in another principle, sometimes hard to come by. Not the solipsist credo that isolates literature from the world outside itself, but the idea of the sovereign integrity of *story*. Authenticity in fiction depends largely on point of view—so it is not Tolstoy's understanding of the shock of history that must be looked for; it is Olenin's. And it is certain that Olenin's mind is altogether bare of anything that will not stir the attention of a dissolute, rich, and copiously indulged young man who lives, like most young men of his kind, wholly in the present, prone to the prejudices of his class and time. Tolstoy means to wake him up—not to history, not to pity or oppression, but to the sublimeness of the natural world.

So come, reader, and never mind!—set aside the somber claims of history, at least for the duration of this airy novel. *A Midsummer Night's Dream* pays no heed to the Spanish Armada; *Pride and Prejudice* happily ignores the Napoleonic Wars; *The Cossacks* is unstained by old terrors. A bucolic fable is under way, and Olenin will soon succumb to the mountains, the forest, the village, the spirited young men, the bold young women. His first view of the horizon—"the massive mountains, clean and white in their gentle contours, the intricate, distinct line of the peaks and the sky"—captivates him beyond his stale expectations, and far more genuinely than the recent enthusiasms of Moscow: "Bach's music or love, neither of which he believed in."

> All his Moscow memories, the shame and repentance, all his foolish and trivial dreams about the Caucasus, disappeared forever. It was as if a solemn voice told him: "Now it has begun!"…Two Cossacks ride by, their rifles in slings bouncing lightly on their backs, and the brown and gray legs of their horses blur—again the mountains. Across the Terek [river], smoke rises from a village—again the mountains. The sun rises and sparkles on the Terek, shimmering through the weeds—again the mountains. A bullock cart rolls out of a Cossack village, the women are walking, beautiful young women—the mountains.

And almost in an instant Olenin is transformed, at least outwardly. He sheds his formal city clothes for a Circassian coat to which a dagger is strapped, grows a Cossack mustache and beard, and carries a Cossack rifle. Even his complexion alters, from an urban pallor to the ruddiness of clear mountain air. After three months of hard bivouac living, the Russian soldiers come flooding into the village, stinking of tobacco, their presence and possessions forced on unwilling Cossack hosts. Olenin is no ordinary soldier—his servant has accompanied him from Moscow, and he is plainly a gentleman who can pay well for his lodging, so he is quartered in one of the better accommodations, a gabled house with a porch, which belongs to the cornet, a man of self-conscious status: he is a teacher attached to the regiment. To make room for him, the cornet and his family must move into an adjacent thatch-roofed cabin: Olenin, like every Russian billeted in the village, is an unwelcome encroachment. "You think I need such a plague? A bullet into your bowels!" cries Old Ulitka, the cornet's wife. Maryanka, the daughter, gives him silent teasing hostile glances, and Olenin yearns to speak to her: "Her strong, youthful step, the untamed look in the flashing eyes peering over the edge of the white kerchief, and her strong, shapely body struck Olenin. . . . 'She is the one!' he thought." And again:

> He watched with delight how freely and gracefully she leaned forward, her pink smock clinging to her breasts and shapely legs, and how she straightened up, her rising breasts outlined clearly beneath the tight cloth. He watched her slender feet lightly touch the ground in their worn slippers, and her strong arms with rolled-up sleeves thrusting the spade into the dung as if in anger, her deep black eyes glancing at him. Though her delicate eyebrows frowned at times, her eyes expressed pleasure and awareness of their beauty.

But he cannot approach her. He is solitary, watchful, bemused by everything around him. He sits on his porch, reading, dreaming; alone and lost in the woods, he is overpowered by a spurt of mystical idealism. More and more the abandoned enticements and impressions of Moscow ebb, and more and more he immerses himself in Cossack habits. He befriends a garrulous, grizzled old hunter, Eroshka, a drunkard and a sponger, who teaches him the secrets of the forest and introduces him to chikhir, the local spirits. In and out of his cups, Eroshka is a rough-cut philosopher, ready to be blood brother to all — Tatars, Armenians, Russians. He mocks the priests, and believes that "when you croak, grass will grow over your grave, and that will be that." "There's no sin in anything," he tells Olenin. "It's all a lie!"

And meanwhile Maryanka continues elusive. She is being courted by Lukashka, whom Olenin both admires and envies. Lukashka is all that Olenin is not — brash, reckless, wild, a fornicator and carouser, fit for action, at one with the life of a fighter. He is a Cossack, and it is a Cossack — not Olenin — that is Maryanka's desire. Even when Olenin is finally and familiarly accepted by Old Ulitka, Maryanka resists. At bottom, *The Cossacks* is an old-fashioned love triangle, as venerable as literature itself; yet it cannot be consummated, on either man's behalf. Maryanka may not have Lukashka — violence destroys him. And she must repudiate Olenin: he is a stranger, and will always remain so. Despite the Circassian coat, despite Eroshka's embraces, despite the merrymaking chikhir, he is, unalterably, a Russian gentleman. He will never be a Cossack. In the end Moscow will reclaim him.

But Tolstoy's art has another purpose, apart from the regretful realism of the tale's denouement and its understated psychological wisdom. It is, in this novel, a young man's art, instinct with ardor — an ardor lacking any tendril of the judgmental. By contrast, the old Tolstoy, at seventy, pledged to religio-political issues of conscience, nevertheless declined to lend his moral weight to a the road leading from the vineyards, and grapes crushed by the wheels lay everywhere in the dust. Little boys and girls, their arms and mouths filled with grapes and their shirts stained with grape juice, ran after their mothers. Tattered laborers carried filled baskets on powerful shoulders. Village girls, kerchiefs wound tightly across their faces, drove bullocks harnessed to local carts. Soldiers by the roadside asked for grapes, and the women climbed into the rolling carts and threw bunches down, the men holding out their shirt flaps to catch them. In some courtyards the grapes were already being pressed, and the aroma of grape-skin leavings filled the air. . . . Laughter, song, and the happy voices of women came from within a sea of shadowy green vines, through which their smocks and kerchiefs peeked.

The scene is Edenic, bursting with fecundity, almost biblical in its overflowingness. Scents and juices spill out of every phrase: it is Tolstoy's sensuous genius at its ripest. Olenin will return to Moscow, yes; but his eyes have been dyed by the grape harvest, and he will never again see as he once saw, before the Caucasus, before Maryanka, before the mountains. The novel's hero is the primordial earth itself, civilization's dream of the pastoral. The old Tolstoy—that crabbed puritanical sermonizing septuagenarian who wrote *What Is Art?*, a tract condemning the pleasures of the senses—might wish to excoriate the twenty-something author of *The Cossacks*. The old Tolstoy is the apostle of renunciation. But the young Tolstoy, who opens Olenin to the intoxications of the natural world, and to the longings of love, means to become, at least for a time, an apostle of desire.

From 1953, when he was twenty-one, to 1975, at forty-three, Updike saw into print one hundred and seven short stories. Four, he reports in a foreword to his ambitiously—or nostalgically—assembled *Early Stories*, have been omitted, leaving one hundred and three. During this same period he published seven novels and five books of poetry. But to marvel at copiousness would be to misconceive achievement: all that arithmetic is, however impressive, beside the point. The stories, after all, came to us quietly, one by one, not in the roaring and multitudinous cascade that is this justifiably prideful collection.

And read one by one, as they first appeared in the pages of a magazine (*The New Yorker*, chiefly), what the stories revealed was the mind of an artist on whom nothing is lost, for whom seeing is fused with the most filigreed turns of language. Updike is a potent stylist, but of a particular kind—less psychological (though he is psychological too), less analytical (though he is frequently that), than visual and painterly. His effects are of sheen and shadow, color and form, spine and splay, hair and haunch. "My main debt," he oddly insists, "which may not be evident, is to Hemingway; it was he who showed us all how much tension and complexity unalloyed dialogue can convey, and how much poetry lurks in the simplest nouns and predicates." One takes this in resistingly. Updike's dialogue is spare and unerring, but nuance and image ride his nouns and verbs in consciously intricate dress; he is far closer to baroque Nabokov than to stripped Hemingway.

The themes that absorb him above all others are eros and God; or the mysteries of women and death. This is quickly manifest, even in the earliest narratives of childhood and youth, set in Updike's native small-town Pennsylvania, with its poignant intimacies of Depression-era families whose autobiographical phases, like elusive moons, are only partly veiled. There is, repeatedly, the impressionable boy, an only child; the affectionate and winning father; the restless, thwarted mother; the mother's aging parents; the move from town to farm—Updike's modestly magical surround, illumined half by memory, half by the maker's craft. But already here, at a New Year's party in "The Happiest I've Been," the nineteen-year-old John Nordholm will learn how the back of a young man's thumb can fit against the curve of a girl's breast, while Updike's scrupulously magnifying notice measures "her two lush eyebrows and then the spaces of skin between the rough curls, some black and some bleached, that fringed her forehead." This preoccupation with the contours of femaleness evolves from story to story, until the arrival, in 1973, of the gentle pornography of "Transaction," wherein a prostitute is accorded the sexual dignity of a wife. Elliptically, the narrator concludes: "What she had given him, delicately, was death."

Some seventy pages before this revelation, David, the much younger protagonist of "Pigeon Feathers," a boy in theological anguish over the inevitability of his own extinction, is coerced into shooting some pigeons in a barn. As they fall lifeless, he observes "the somehow effortless mechanics of the feathers . . . no two alike, designs executed, it seemed, in a controlled rapture," while Updike rises to one of his most remarked-on sentences— or call it the sentence that confirmed his precocious fame: "He was robed in this certainty: that the God who had lavished such craft upon these worthless birds would not destroy His whole Creation by refusing to let David live forever."

Like many of these fictions, both early and late, "Pigeon Feathers" is structured on an arc: from the commonplace (the birds in the barn) to a crisis of realization (the promise of an afterlife). The trajectory may be predictable, but the juxtapositions are not. In "The Music School," for example, the flow is from the material consistency of the eucharistic wafer to the murder of a computer expert; from a daughter's piano lessons to an intimation of adultery; from the plot of an abandoned novel to a visit to a psychiatrist, and finally to a communal confession at a worship service. In this contrapuntal narrative stream, there is more than one coda to decode; but one note is struck more deliberately than any other: "We are all pilgrims, faltering toward divorce." And where there is divorce, there is marriage; and where there is marriage, there are children. The everyday seizes Updike's tireless gaze—babies, adolescents, couples, sometimes in stasis, as in genre painting, sometimes kinetic, like the swoop of a thought. As his heroes age, the hot empathy that flooded the boy and the youth grows objectively cool. In "Solitaire," a man on the verge of divorce ricochets between two women: "His mistress cried big: with thrilling swiftness her face dissolved and, her mouth smeared all out of shape, she lurched against him with an awkward bump and soaked his throat in abusive sobs. Whereas his wife wept like a miraculous icon, her face immobile while the tears ran." Portraits inscribed in ice.

What is notable, and curious, in Updike is that his sexual scenes seem as distanced and skeptical as a lapsed seminarian's meticulously recited breviary, while his God-seeking passages send out orgasmic shudders, whether of exaltation or distress. In "The Deacon," a decaying old wooden church—rotted wiring, warped boards, leaky ceiling, worn hymnals, superannuated remnants of congregants—is nevertheless instinct with holy ardor, and with a kind of intergalactic loneliness. "Lifeguard," a celebrated fiction written by a young man still in his twenties, is an extended, if lyrical, religious pun: crosses abound, the red cross on the lifeguard's tall chair, "the pale X on the back of the overall-wearing mason or carpenter." The lifeguard is a divinity student;

his task is to be saved, and to save. "Women," he reflects, observing the "breeding swarm" half-naked in bathing suits, "are an alien race of pagans set down among us. Every seduction is a conversion." His mission is to "lift the whole mass into immortality." The story's symptomatic crossover is this overlapping of flesh and redemption, so that one may be induced to permeate the other. It is how Updike reconciles the social bustle of ordinary lives with the rapturous aloneness of faith.

His is not a social faith. Though "Lifeguard" closes with an exhortation to "be joyful," the Kierkegaardian singleness of the God-possessed, quivering among the darker stars, predominates. This singleness, this historyless aloneness, turns up in the essayistic aperçus and musings and final exhalations that thread through both plot and plotlessness, alongside the daily vernacular, between, so to speak, the acts. The acts are tremendously variegated; in the spacious precincts of eight hundred and more pages, human faces teem, landscapes and interiors are elegiacally documented, a thousand three-dimensional objects cast realistic shadows, time is phosphorescent, moods coagulate and dissolve. Updike owns the omnivorous faculty of seeing the telltale flame in every mundane gesture. Despite this busy Brueghelian amplitude, the concluding soliloquy of the unsettled young husband in "The Astronomer," who is befuddled by an atheistic sophist, carries a recognizable Updikean signature: "What is the past, after all, but a vast sheet of darkness in which a few moments, pricked apparently at random, shine?"

But the past, so defined, is not the same as history. Only compare the early fiction of Saul Bellow, where history infiltrates nearly every thought or movement—which is perhaps why Bellow has been called our most "European" novelist. Among contemporary fiction writers, Updike is the most rootedly American (though of German, not WASP, stock), and the most self-consciously Protestant: the individual in singular engagement with God. The Protestant idea of God, which nurtured and shaped America, is the narrowed Lord of persons, not of hosts; He is not conspicuously the Lord of history. This may be the reason the Nobel literary committee, afloat on the turbulent waves of vast historical grievances, has so far overlooked Updike. (At the 1986 International PEN Congress, presided over by Norman Mailer and titled "The Writer's Imagination and the Imagination of the State," while angry literary politicos stormed against the perfidies of governments, America's in particular, Updike spoke in quiet praise of his own relation to the state: the dependable USA mailbox.)

It may be that the absence of a brooding and burdensome history in these stories accounts for the luxuriance of their lyrical andantes. Here are lives essentially tranquil, unharried by turmoil and threat beyond the extrusions of plaintively aspiring passions. There may be local and topical distractions, but by and large Updike's scenes and characters express a propitious America, mottled only by metaphysical ruminations. If, as Adorno tells us, there can be no poetry after Auschwitz, possibly the converse is true: poetry belongs to the trustful calm that is the negation of Auschwitz—and which, at its bountiful heart, is Updike's witty and incandescent America. Two generations of readers and writers have been awed by Updike's rhapsodic powers and the opulent resources of his language; still, there are occasional complaints of excess, of bedizened satiety. "A seigneurial gratuity," James Wood calls it, "as if language were a meaningless bill to a very rich man." Updike is assuredly rich in language (its dazzle is tempered by colloquial rushes of dialogue), and if his fictive world is poor in the sorrows of history, if the only conflagrations his characters must witness are picnic fires, it is no wonder, and mainly a pleasure, that he turns to the elaborations of imagery. Bech, Updike's alter ego in "The Bulgarian Poetess," remarks to an enchanting woman fettered by Communism—the closest this collection comes to a tyrannical age—"It is a matter of earnest regret that you and I must live on opposite sides of the world." In light of the imperial craft of Updike's ambitious twenties and thirties, it must be, rather, a matter of felicitous relief. The America of these early stories may be the mostly untrammeled land we remember; but language in all its fecundity is Updike's native country, and he is its patriot.

THROWING AWAY THE CLEF:
SAUL BELLOW'S RAVELSTEIN

ROMAN À CLEF? Never mind. When it comes to novels, the author's life is nobody's business. A novel, even when it is autobiographical, is not an autobiography. If the writer himself leaks the news that such-and-such a character is actually so-and-so in real life, readers nevertheless have an obligation—fiction's enchanted obligation—to shut their ears and turn away. A biographer may legitimately wish to look to *Buddenbrooks*, say, to catch certain tonalities of Thomas Mann's early years; a reader is liberated from the matching game. Fiction is subterranean, not terrestrial. Or it is like Tao: say what it is, and that is what it is not. One reason to read imaginative literature is to be carried off into the strangeness of an unknown planet, not to be dogged by the verifiable facts of this one. Why should we care for blunt information —for those ephemeral figures fictional creatures are "based on"? The originals vanish; their simulacra, powerful marvels, endure. Does it matter that "The Rape of the Lock" makes sport of one Arabella Fermor and of the eminent Lord Petre? Fermor and Petre are bones. Belinda and Sir Plume go on frolicking from line to frothy line of Pope's comic ode. Who lives forever—Flimnap, the all-important treasurer of the Kingdom of Lilliput, or his sent-up model, Sir Robert Walpole, gone to dust two and a half centuries ago? Why should Philip Roth's "Philip Roth" be Philip Roth?

And why should Saul Bellow's Ravelstein be Allan Bloom? Or, to turn the question around (the better to get at an answer), why should Saul Bellow's Ravelstein *not* be Allan Bloom? It might be argued that Bellow has a fat track record of insinuating into his fiction the frenziedly brilliant men he has known, intellectuals given to complications: in *Humboldt's Gift*, Delmore Schwartz; in "Zetland: By a Character Witness," Isaac Rosenfeld; in "What Kind of Day Did You Have?," Harold Rosenberg. And in *Ravelstein*, Allan Bloom, Bellow's longtime colleague at the University of Chicago's School of Social Thought. But Bloom and Bellow were more entangled—more raveled—than academic colleagues usually are: they were cognitive companions, mutual brain-pickers, and, in Bloom's Platonic lingo, true friends. For Bloom especially, friendship was a calling, "the community of those who seek the truth, the potential knowers." In 1987, Bellow supplied a foreword to *The Closing of the American Mind*, Bloom's startling bestseller—startling because it *was* a bestseller, despite its countless invocations of Socrates, Herodotus, Nietzsche, Hobbes, Locke, Descartes, Spinoza, Bacon, Newton, and all the other denizens of the philosophical mind. Summing up Bloom, Bellow faithfully reported, "Professor Bloom is neither a debunker nor a satirist, and his conception of seriousness carries him far beyond the positions of academia"—and then ran off the Bloomian rails to tumble into engaging self-clarification. With familiar antic Bellovian bounce, Bellow wrote, "There was not a chance in the world that Chicago, with the agreement of my eagerly Americanizing extended family, would make me in its image. Before I was capable of thinking clearly, my resistance to its material weight took the form of obstinacy. I couldn't say why I would not allow myself to become the product of an *environment*. But gainfulness, utility, prudence, business, had no hold on me. My mother wanted me to be a fiddler, or, failing that, a rabbi." (He became, in a way, both: a fiddler with the sharps and flats of American prose, and a metaphysical ruminator.) Bloom, too, in the final pages of his book, spoke of living "independent of accidents, of circumstance"—a view, Bellow affirmed, that was "the seed from which my life grew."

Two self-propelled thinkers, freed from predictive forces. They had in common an innate longing, revealed in youth, for the bliss of Idea. Bloom, under the head "From Socrates' *Apology* to Heidegger's *Rektoratsrede*": "When I was fifteen years old I saw the University of Chicago for the first time and somehow sensed that I had discovered my life." The university, he early came to understand, "provided an atmosphere of free inquiry, and therefore excluded what is not conducive to or is inimical to such inquiry. It made a distinction between what is important and not important. It protected the tradition, not because tradition is tradition but because tradition provides models of discussion on a uniquely high level. It contained marvels and made possible friendships consisting in shared experiences of those marvels." And Bellow, spilling the beans among the wayward paragraphs of his foreword: "Reluctantly my father allowed me at seventeen to enter the university, where I was an enthusiastic (wildly excited) but erratic and contrary student. If I signed up for Economics 201, I was sure to spend all my time reading Ibsen and Shaw. Registering for a poetry course, I was soon bored by meter and stanzas, and shifted my attention to Kropotkin's *Memoirs of a Revolutionist* and Lenin's *What Is to Be Done? . . .* I preferred to read poetry on my own without the benefit of lectures on the caesura." Both young men are "wildly excited" by this opening into the seductions of ultimate meaning. One becomes an extraordinary teacher. The other becomes Saul Bellow. One writes the cardboard sentences, workmanlike and often mentally exhilarating, of the intellectual nonwriter. The other *writes.* For years, until Bloom's death, the two are true friends—a friendship bred in Chicago, with robust tendrils stretching toward ancient Athens and the dustiness of upper Broadway. Bloom, like the Ravelstein of Bellow's novel, is in thrall to Socrates. Like Ravelstein, he publishes a volume critical of the displacement of humanist liberal culture by the pieties of political cant. Like Ravelstein, he earns a fortune from his book and feels the venom of the radical left. Like Ravelstein, he is a homosexual who reveres eros and scorns gay rights; again like Ravelstein, he has a Chinese lover. This ought to be more than enough to make the case for Ravelstein as roman à clef. But there is no case. Or: to make the case in so literal a fashion, one on one (on all fours, as lawyers put it), is to despise the idea of the novel—the principle of what a novel is—and to harbor a private lust to destroy it.

In scary-kitschy old movies, an ambition-crazed scientist constructs in his laboratory two ominously identical boxes, in the shape of telephone booths, side by side. He enters one, the door shuts, a fearful electrical buzz follows, lights flash and darken, and suddenly the first box is empty and the scientist stands, intact, in the other: a triumph of molecular disintegration and reintegration; instant transportation sans trolley or rocket. If you are ready to believe this, you will accept the notion of roman à clef—that a life is transferable from flesh to print; that since the resemblances line up ever so nicely, Ravelstein "is" Bloom. Under this persuasion, fiction is hijacked by gossip, the vapor of transience. Under this persuasion, Bellow's own admission (he has confirmed that his model was Bloom) invites the scandal of outing: Ravelstein dies of AIDS; then did Bloom, who never intimated having the disease, die of it? Under this persuasion, Andrew Sullivan, noted gay journalist and pundit, observes how salutary it is that even a conservative like Bloom can be openly gay. Bloom's politics, enemies, sexual habits, even his dying, are all freshly rehearsed — because Ravelstein is Bloom.

Ravelstein is not Bloom. To insist on it is hardly to allow Bloom to speak for himself in what is left of him. Bloom, dead, is (as a doctor once described to me the condition of a newly deceased relative) a pile of electrons. Bloom, still lively, continues his worthy arguments in teacherly discourses that, far from staling, have intensified at a time when dot-com merges with New Age. Say of Bloom what Bloom said of Leo Strauss, his venerated philosophy professor: that he "left his own memorial in the body of works in which what he understood to be his essence lives on." Say this; but not that Bellow has written Bloom. That Bellow acknowledges Bloom as his subject — acknowledges it with all the authority of the mighty *New York Times* behind him — means nothing, or almost nothing, in the kingdom of the novel. An author's extraliterary utterance (blunt information), prenovel or postnovel, may infiltrate journalism; it cannot touch the novel itself. Fiction does not invent out of a vacuum, but it *invents;* and what it invents is, first, the fabric and cadence of language, and then a slant of idea that sails out of these as a fin lifts from the sea. The art of the novel (worn yet opulent phrase) is in the mix of idiosyncratic language — language imprinted in the writer, like the whorl of the fingertip — and an unduplicable design inscribed on the mind by character and image. Invention has little capacity for the true-to-life snapshot. It is true to its own stirrings. The real-life Bloom, steeped in a congeries of arresting social propositions, lacked language and metaphor — which is why the legacy of his books can replicate his thought, but not the mysterious crucible of his breath.

Bellow, in going after his friend's mystery, leaves Bloom behind—just as in past novels and stories he ultimately deserts Rosenberg, Rosenfeld, and Schwartz, those latter-day piles of electrons, who, like Bloom, are obliged to live on, impressively enough, in the ink of their own fingerprints. Bellow's is an independent art. The souls who thrive or shrivel in his fiction ("soul" being his most polemical term) are not replicas; they are primal coinages, unbounded by flesh and likely to be faithless to fact. Literary verisimilitude is a chimera. Look to the "stein" in Ravelstein for a suggestive clue: the philosopher's stone that turns base metal into gold. Allan Bloom, Bellow's supremely intelligent Chicago compatriot, had the university professor's usual tin ear for prose (his own). But the philosopher's stone does not mimic or reproduce; it transmutes. Bloom's tin is Ravelstein's gold.

"Lifestyle" raised to a right equal to other human rights was what Bloom particularly excoriated; such relativism, he believed, led to "nihilism as moralism." Andrew Sullivan sizes up Bloom acutely when he remarks that "victimology never tempted him." Sullivan speculates that Bloom's homosexuality "may even have reinforced his conservatism," a striking aside—but what is it doing in the context of Bellow's novel? An essay on Bloom ought to be an essay on Bloom. It is important to repudiate the tag of roman à clef not only because it is careless and rampant, but because it reduces and despoils the afflatus—and the freedom—of the literary imagination. The clef gets stuck in the lock, and the lock attaches to fetters.

§

And so to the real Ravelstein of the novel. I am reluctant to speak of Bellow's "voice," a writerly term overgrown with academic fungus, and by now nearly useless. (Consider also the ruination by English departments of "gaze," that magical syllable, fully and foully theorized into ash.) Better to return to Bellow's mother, who hoped for a fiddling son; better to think of him as a sentence-and-paragraph fiddler, or a rabbi presiding over an unruly congregation of words. The words are unruly because they refuse to be herded into categories of style: they are high, low, shtick, soft-shoe, pensive, mystical, sermonic, eudaemonic—but never catatonic; always on the move, in the swim, bathed in some electricity-conducting effluvium. Bellow's incremental sound—or noise —rejects imitation the way the human immune system will reject foreign tissue. There are no part-Bellows or next-generation Bellows; there are no literary descendants. As for precursors, Bellow's jumpy motor has more in common (while not so fancy) with the engine that ratchets Gerard Manley Hopkins's lines—that *run-run-turn-stop!*—than with any prose ancestor. In *Ravelstein* he puts these racing weight-bearing energies to use in something that ought not to be called a "portrait." ("What an olden-days' word 'portraying' has become," says Chick, the novel's narrator.) Verbal sculpture is more like it—think of those Roman busts with strong noses and naked heads, round heavy stone on square heavy plinths. Ravelstein's head is central, tactile, dominant, and it is examined with a sculptor's or architect's eye. "On his bald head you felt that what you were looking at were the finger marks of its shaper." "This tall pin- or chalk-striped dude with his bald head (you always felt there was something dangerous about its whiteness, its white force, its dents) . . ." "He liked to raise his long arms over the light gathered on his bald head and give a comic cry." "There are bald heads that proclaim their strength. Ravelstein's head had been like that." "His big eyes were concentrated in that bald, cranial watchtower of his." "You couldn't imagine an odder container for his odd intellect. Somehow his singular, total, almost geological baldness implied that there was nothing hidden about him." "The famous light of Paris was concentrated on his bald head." And so on, image upon image. Ravelstein's is not so much a man's head as it is a lit dome: the dome (or Renaissance *duomo*) of some high-ceilinged cathedral or broad-corridored library. Ravelstein's ideas—also his gossip, his extravagant wants—are solidly housed. This head is no hotel for brief mental sojourns.

A hotel is where we first meet Abe Ravelstein—the lavish penthouse of the Hotel Crillon, in Paris, where the luxury-intoxicated humanities professor, "who only last year had been a hundred thousand dollars in debt," is reveling in the millions piled up by his cultural bestseller. Ravelstein is a sybarite. He is also a man who would know the Greek origin of that word. His appetite for five-thousand-dollar designer suits, silk ties, gold pens, mink quilts, French crystal, smuggled Cuban cigars, Oriental carpets, antique sideboards, and all the other paraphernalia of the dedicated voluptuary, is accompanied by a philosopher's scrupulous worship of civic virtue. Ravelstein is a principled atheist, a homosexual (but quietly, privately), a bit of a matchmaker, a thinker "driven by longing"—a longing understood as Aristophanes meant it, the haunted desire for human completion. He likes puns and gags, he likes meddling in the lives of his brightest students, he likes being ahead of the news (thanks to former students now in high places); his cell phone is at the ready. Socrates is his ideal and Thucydides his immediacy, but he is as alert to current anti-Semitic subtleties and historic anti-Jewish depredations as he is to the problems of Alcibiades in the Sicilian campaign of the Peloponnesian War. Chick—the not-so-famous midlist writer who is Ravelstein's catch-as-catch-can biographer—seizes his subject at the crux: "He preferred Athens, but he respected Jerusalem greatly."

Commenting and kibitzing in the first person, Chick (a self-described "serial marrier") mostly keeps a low profile, except in the matter of his wives: Vela, the vengeful Romanian physicist who walks out on him, and Rosamund, the loyal, intelligent, empathic young woman who was once Ravelstein's student. Other characters pass, or hurtle, through Chick's recording cascades: Nikki, Ravelstein's presumed lover, "a handsome, smooth-skinned, black-haired, Oriental, graceful, boyish man," for whom Ravelstein buys a chestnut-colored BMW with kid-leather upholstery; Rachmiel Kogon, "tyrannically fixated, opinionated," a genuine ex-Oxonian don but a fake Brit, owner of complete sets of Dickens, James, Hume, and Gibbon; Morris Herbst, an observant Jew with a heart transplant obtained from the deadly crash of a goyish motorcyclist in Missouri; Radu Grielescu, a renowned Jungian mythologist and Nazi-tainted former Iron Guardist, who play-acts blameless politesse; Battle, paratrooper, pilot, ballroom dancer, Sanskrit scholar, with "the mouth of a Celtic king." They represent, in Chick's phrase, "penetrations of the external world." Accounting for them to the impatient Ravelstein—who recommends a larger concern for society and politics—Chick argues, "I had no intention . . . of removing, by critical surgery, the metaphysical lenses I was born with."

It is these powerful lenses that finally raise questions about how a novel—generically, *the* novel—is to be fathomed. *Ravelstein* is busy with revelatory incident but is mainly plotless: Ravelstein becomes ill, rallies, retains his acerbic nobility, declines further, and begins the slide into death. At Ravelstein's hospital bedside Chick uncovers the mundane secret of the philosopher's eloquent cranial dome. "Now and then I put my hand to my friend's bald head," he confides. ". . . I was surprised to find that there was an invisible stubble on his scalp. He seemed to have decided that total baldness suited him better than thinning hair, and shaved his head as well as his cheeks. Anyway," Chick concludes, "this head was rolling toward the grave." A mightiness theatricalized by the razor's artifice; a mightiness at last undone. Following which, Rosamund and Chick vacation in the Caribbean ("one huge tropical slum," Chick characterizes these islands), where he eats spoiled fish and nearly perishes from the effects of poisoning; Rosamund's intrepid devotion through an extended medical ordeal saves him. This final occurrence, the novel's climactic scene, seems out of kilter with the rich thick Ravelstein stew that precedes it. Chick's preoccupations veer off the Ravelsteinian tracks into the demands of his own circumstances, much as Bellow, in his foreword to Bloom's blockbuster, ran off the Bloomian rails to grapple with his own spirit. But by now Ravelstein is dead; and a novel is not a biography. Biographies are innately saddled with structure. When the biographer's subject dies, the biography comes to a close—what else can it choose to do? A novel need make no such obeisance to graph or sine curve, or to the deeper curve of death's scythe. Only the lower orders of fiction—case solved, romance consummated—abide by ordained rigidities and patterns. The literary novel (call it the artist's novel) engenders freedom, flexibility, exemption from determined outcomes; waywardness and surprise. What falls out then is not story (or not only story), but certain obstinacies and distillations, which can be inspected solely through Chick's metaphysical lenses. It can even be argued that it is only through this supra-optical equipment that fiction's necessary enactments can be prodded into lustiness.

What "metaphysical" intends is not left unspecified: it is the earthly shock of Creation's plenitude. "Ordinary daily particulars were my specialty," Chick explains. "The heart of things is shown in the surface of those things." Elsewhere he illustrates: "I carried [Rosamund] through the water, the sand underfoot ridged as the surface of the sea was rippled, and inside the mouth the hard palate had its ridges too." Out of the blue, the ridges of the hard palate! A planetary connectedness, a Darwinian propensity for minute perceiving—which Ravelstein, whose thought runs vertically through history, both marvels at and chides. Here Rosamund sides with her old teacher: "But this is how you do things, Chick: the observations you make crowd out the main point." They are discussing Grielescu, the concealed Iron Guardist. "How could such a person be politically dangerous?" Chick counters. "His jacket cuffs come down over his knuckles." An instant of comic toughness, reminiscent of the famous crack in *Augie March*: "He had rich blood. His father peddled apples." But Grielescu, a minor character, barely a walk-on, is the novel's suboceanic mover: he is like the ridges of the hard palate inside the mouth. Once you become conscious of these shallow bumps, you cannot leave off exploring them—they lead you mentally to the treacherous floor of the deepest sea. In Ravelstein's exuberant mind-roving prime, his memoirist recalls, he had been absorbed in nasty speculations about Grielescu's Nazi past: how Grielescu had been summoned to lecture in Jerusalem, and how the invitation was soon withdrawn. Weakening now, under death's lintel, Ravelstein appears to be enveloped in Jewish fate, in the twentieth century's "great evil." What was once a flicker in a crepuscular background, veiled by a Greek passion for polis and eros, invades and illumines his still pulsing intellect. "It was unusual for him these days, in any conversation, to mention Plato or even Thucydides. He was full of Scripture now," Chick records. "In his last days it was the Jews he wanted to talk about, not the Greeks."

Athens gives way to Jerusalem—but it is understood, anyhow, that Socrates had always been Ravelstein's rebbe, and Periclean Athens his yeshiva. Ravelstein's final dictum: in the wake of "such a volume of hatred and the denial of the right to live," Jews are "historically witness to the absence of redemption." For the reader looking back on Ravelstein's musings as preserved by Chick, a great totting-up looms. Of a French landlord's ancestry: "Those Gabineaus were famous Jew-haters." Of Grielescu's myth expertise: "The Jews had better understand their status with respect to myth. Why should they have any truck with myth? It was myth that demonized them." Of Jews and teaching: "We are a people of teachers. For millennia, Jews have taught and been taught. Without teaching, Jewry was an impossibility." Of a luncheon for T. S. Eliot, where the snooty hostess complains of Ravelstein's manners: "She wasn't going to let any kike behave badly at her table." And again: "And what will T. S. Eliot think of us!"

That last gibe is to the point. How would T. S. Eliot assess an American novelist (one of those "freethinking Jews" he deplored) so confident of writer's sovereignty that he can fiddle with the English language with all the freewheeling relish of an Elizabethan inventing new inflections—and in such a way as to make *The Waste Land* (and, God knows, those solemnified essays and plays) seem lethargic? "I had a Jewish life to lead in the American language," Chick announces, "and that's not a language that's helpful with dark thoughts." But it is through Chick's dark thoughts—and not only Ravelstein's—that we are apprised, or reminded, of Lloyd George's, Kipling's, and Voltaire's hot anti-Semitism, and of "the Wehrmacht way of getting around responsibility for their crimes," and of German militarism as "the bloodiest and craziest kind of revanchist murderous zeal." This is a long way from Rachel née Rabinovitch's murderous paws, and it is also a substantial distance from the mannerly fear of nomenclature that paradoxically turned Nathan Weinstein into the ferocious Nathanael West. Sovereignty for a novelist means unleashing the language of one's marrow and—this especially—tunneling into any subject matter, however transgressive it may be of the current societal glyph. (Think of that other Bloom as *echt* Dubliner. And note that Ravelstein's snooty hostess is named Mrs. Glyph.) Hence Chick's reflections on leading a Jewish life in the American language are light-years from the rivalrous group-tenets of multiculturalism, and ought not to be mistaken for them. The reviewer who called *Ravelstein* "Bellow's most Jewish novel" is only partly right; on second thought, if he means it as essence or circumscription, he is all wrong. It is not the nature of subject matter that defines a novel. It is the freedom to be at home in any subject matter; and this holds for Louis Auchincloss as much as it holds for Saul Bellow. All subject matter is equal under the law (or democratic lawlessness) of the novel. What is a novel? A persuasion toward dramatic interiority. A word-hoard that permits its inventor to stand undefined, unprescribed, liberated from direction or coercion. Freedom makes sovereignty; it is only when the writer is unfettered by external expectations that clarity of character—Ravelstein, for instance, bald and baldly opinionated, intellectually quarrelsome, a comic epicurean, a hospitable thinker with trembling hands, a Jew tormented by evil and pedagogically fixed on virtue—can be imagined into being. When, apropos of Bloom's 1987 credo, Bellow insisted that "I would not allow myself to become the product of an *environment*," he had a canny interest in those italics. As for the idea of roman à clef: what is it if not the product, and the imprisoning imposition, of an environment?

WASHINGTON SQUARE:
SO MANY ABSENT THINGS

HENRY JAMES CAME TO PARIS in the bright autumn of 1879, intending to enjoy a visit with Turgenev and then go on to Florence. But early in December a ferocious blizzard assaulted northern Europe; the roads to Italy were closed off, and Paris lay encased in alpine snow drifts. Confined to the snug fireside of his hotel room, James wrote—in one sitting, almost fifteen thousand words!—the slyly comical little "international" tale "A Bundle of Letters," which scrambled Americans abroad in a mix of bewildered Europeans. Though James was by now permanently settled in London, traveling intermittently in France and Italy, America was never far from his reflections. During the previous September he had completed his long study of Hawthorne, with its notorious condemnation of his native land:

> No sovereign, no court, no personal loyalty, no aristocracy, no church, no clergy, no army, no diplomatic service, no country gentlemen, no palaces, no castles, nor manors, nor old country-houses, nor parsonages, nor thatched cottages nor ivied ruins; no cathedrals, nor abbeys, nor little Norman churches; no great Universities nor public schools—no Oxford, nor Eton, nor Harrow; no literature, no novels, no museums, no pictures, no political society, no sporting class—no Epsom nor Ascot!

So many "absent things," he concluded, "upon an English or a French imagination, would probably as a general thing be appalling." All this implied that James—an expatriate, after all—was equally appalled at how little America had to offer his own imagination. Yet in the same essay he tellingly qualified these objections: "It is on manners, customs, usages, habits, forms, upon all these things matured and established, that a novelist lives—they are the very stuff his work is made of." Such stuff, he argued, could be found even in America: "The American knows that a good deal remains." In the winter of 1880, sheltered from the storms of Paris, he conceived his most American fiction—a novel of manners and customs, altogether barren of castles and ivied ruins, and set mainly in the front parlor of a New York brownstone in the early decades of the nineteenth century. He named it *Washington Square*, after a neighborhood redolent of his own childhood. Momentarily straying from the grain of the narrative, and invoking memory and reverie in a "topographical parenthesis," he recalls that it was in this place long ago, "as you might have been informed on good authority,"

> that you had come into a world which appeared to offer a variety of sources of interest; it was here that your grandmother lived, in venerable solitude, and dispensed a hospitality which commended itself alike to the infant imagination and the infant palate; it was here that you took your first walks abroad, following the nurserymaid with unequal step, and sniffing up the strange odor of the ailanthus trees which at that time formed the principal umbrage of the Square, and diffused an aroma that you were not yet critical enough to dislike as it deserved; it was here, finally, that your first school, kept by a broad-bosomed, broad-based old lady with a ferule, who was always having tea in a blue cup, with a saucer that didn't

match, enlarged the circle both of your observations and your sensations.

The digression is crucial. It points to a novel of absences—and not only of abbeys and thatched cottages. To write it, James absented himself from Paris, enduring a choppy Channel crossing, and returned to the confiding familiarity of his London flat. It was a stroke of self-possession. What he possessed, or repossessed, were the decisive absences of his own life: the Washington Square of his small boyhood, ripe for retrieval; America, self-driven into willing absence, except for the distant yet persistent pressure of his relations. William, James's older brother—older by more than a year—had recently married. Contemplating the urgent absence of such an eventuality in his own future, James congratulated the new husband with a brother's cautious defensiveness and a novelist's enlarging empathy: "I believe almost as much in marriage for other people as I believe in it little for myself—which," he added, "is saying a good deal."

He believed in matrimony (and its absence) also as a primary subject for the novel as a form: the novel of usages and habits. Of the four major presences, and one minor one, who govern the action of *Washington Square*, three are widowed, and much the worse for it. Dr. Sloper is embittered because he has lost a rich and beautiful and clever wife who has left him a plain and unprepossessing daughter. Mrs. Penniman, the doctor's widowed sister, childless and unoccupied, expends her store of perilous energy on intrigues and flighty romancings. Mrs. Montgomery, the minor presence, a respectable young widow with many children, lives tidily on little money, burdened by a ne'er-do-well brother. For all these deprived persons, the novel—like its author—admits to a belief in the social advantages of matrimony. Had Dr. Sloper's wife not died, he would have continued to enjoy an adored and sprightly companion; as it is, he has only Catherine, the daughter he regards as irredeemably dull. Were Mr. Penniman still alive, Lavinia Penniman's fantasies and shallow mischiefs might sufficiently divert her clergyman husband, who presumably was not averse to having a silly wife to wag a silver tongue at. As for poor Mrs. Montgomery, who knows how a robust man in the house would have disposed of Morris Townsend, her shamelessly sponging brother? All these long-absent spouses, and their clear domestic benefits, foreshadow the husband that will always be absent in Catherine's story.

Catherine Sloper, at twenty-two, is an heiress. Her father, by means of a strenuously fashionable practice, has grown rich; her dead mother, an heiress herself, was richer still. No wonder, then, that a decades-old Hollywood film made from *Washington Square*—Olivia de Havilland soberly regal in period silks—is melodramatically called *The Heiress*. The novel itself is melodrama, recognizably stereotyped in a venerably fixed pattern: a young woman courted by a blatantly charming fortune hunter, an angry father determined to thwart the match. Nor was James unaware of the well-trodden nature of his material. "I am almost a father in an old-fashioned novel," he has Dr. Sloper say, and Morris Townsend, questioned about his prospects, is made to remark, "I have nothing but my good right arm, as they say in the melodramas"—authorial self-consciousness here awkwardly tripping on its skirts. James loses no time, moreover, in presenting the handsome suitor as an attractive but manipulative scoundrel; Morris Townsend's aims are evident nearly from the first. Even Mrs. Penniman's role harks back to the ancient typology of the meddlesome go-between. James's narrative schemes, especially those that touch on a marriage, often enough rely on similar melodrama. *The Portrait of a Lady*, which directly follows *Washington Square*, allows the heiress to wed the scoundrel, thanks to the machinations of the go-between. But Gilbert Osmond is a darkly sinister villain; Morris Townsend is as light and transparent as air.

At bottom, what can these acknowledged contrivances mean for James's art? What we call plot, and he called the fructifying "germ" of the tale, is mostly beside the point. Leon Edel, James's foremost biographer, informs us that James got the idea for *Washington Square* from an anecdote told to him by Mrs. Fanny Kemble, a celebrated actress of the time. "Her brother," Edel recounts, "had jilted an heiress when he discovered that her father would disinherit the girl." But James's sources went deeper than anecdote, or germ, or plot, and deeper surely than the classical arrangements of sentimental drama. It was the jilting that drew him — jilting as flight, a thing James knew well. Putting an ocean behind him, he had jilted America. Fearing the responsibility of tending sickness, he had in effect abandoned his much-loved but tubercular young cousin, Minny Temple, who begged to follow him to Europe. He periodically deserted Constance Woolson, a novelist (and admirer) with whom he kept up a secret friendship; he dreaded the possibility of misperception, hers or the world's. Convivial as he was, sympathetic as he might be, his public life was a series of subtly executed relinquishments and escapes — from attachments unwanted, from ministrations imposed (as when he angrily discovered that Edith Wharton, whose novels were bestsellers, had charitably — and clandestinely — arranged for her publisher to transfer to James a portion of her own royalties). And once he was himself jilted, in a manner of speaking, through William's marriage — William, almost a twin, close in age, close in childhood experience, close in fraternal rivalry. (Leon Edel calls it a "divorce.")

So *Washington Square*, written not long after that marriage, is not only about an actual jilting; it is—in terms of fictive form— an act of literary jilting. It is a novel through which James escapes from the melodramatic frame that engaged him—the archetypes of faithless suitor and unforgiving father, the old lore of innocence wronged. James exploits all of these, and then throws them over. Nor is it simply that he jettisons familiar bathetic tropisms. The frame itself is wrung free of expectation and twisted out of all recognition. There is neither relief nor release; the protagonists are chained to what their innate characteristics of mind have wrought. What begins as melodrama ends as tragedy.

Dr. Sloper is a satirist. Under his cleverly penetrating eye every object, every person, is bound to wither. His delight is to expose the truth, so long as the truth is hurtful. His sister fears him. His daughter reveres him. When the barbs fly, Catherine is mild, meekly withdrawing; it will be a long time before she can admit to her father's cruelty. She cannot satisfy him. No one, he tells himself, "will ever be in love with Catherine . . . poor Catherine isn't romantic." She lacks brilliance, she lacks taste; or, rather, a taste akin to his own: "It made him fairly grimace, in private, to think that a child of his should be both ugly and overdressed." He thinks this "in private," but aloud he is brutal. At a party, observing his daughter's lavish dress, he exclaims, "Is it possible that this magnificent person is my child?" And then, still more cuttingly: "You look as if you had eighty thousand a year."

He is not alone in this evaluation. Morris Townsend, catching sight of the plain young woman in the dress heralding eighty thousand a year, glimpses an opportunity. But if he is a mercenary adventurer, he is something else as well: he can entertain, he can amuse, he can entrance. By way of approaching Catherine, he charms Mrs. Penniman, a woman who is too easily charmed. Dr. Sloper is decidedly not charmed. Until just lately, Morris "had been knocking about the world, and living in queer corners"; at present he is living with, and on, his needy sister. His manner is facile, his conversation sprightly:

> Catherine had never heard anyone—especially a young man —talk just like that. It was the way a young man might talk in a novel, or, better still, in a play, on the stage, close before the footlights, looking at the audience and with everyone looking at him, so that you wondered at his presence of mind. And yet Mr. Townsend was not like an actor; he seemed so sincere, so natural.

It is Catherine who is sincere and natural. She is innately diffident, but she is also unassumingly direct. Toward her father she is adoring and humble. The skills of deception are far from her character. Her character: the shrewdly cynical Dr. Sloper believes he is in command of her every trait and limitation—"poor Catherine isn't romantic." And further: "He had moments of irritation at having produced a commonplace child." Yet the unromantic and commonplace child is, despite all, attracted to imaginative influence; she senses that Morris is exactly this—a work of art. When she looks at him she is reminded of novels and plays, of paintings and sculpture.

> He had features like young men in pictures; Catherine had never seen such features—so delicate, so chiseled and finished—among the young New Yorkers whom she passed in the streets and met at dancing parties. He was tall and slim, but he looked extremely strong. Catherine thought that he looked like a statue.

Morris is a work of art; he is also an artist. Like a painter or a novelist, he can create a young woman who never before existed. He can transform Catherine, to whom no one has ever shown honest affection, into a woman who for the first time feels herself to be worthy of love. Always she has abided by her father's low valuation of a weak child without spirit. Morris enchants her with an unforeseen portrait, that of an effulgent figure capable of the ardors of happiness; he has fashioned her, for the moment, into yet another work of art—a golden bride in the morning of life.

Gold—the absence of gold—interferes. Dr. Sloper sees in Morris only the canny maneuvers of a man after money and ease. He abuses him unremittingly: Morris is "a vulgar nature," "extremely insinuating," "a plausible coxcomb," "a selfish idler." Coldly, he informs Catherine that he will disinherit her should she defy him by marrying Townsend. Whereupon Morris, persuaded finally of the force of this intention, disappears—precisely as Dr. Sloper, with all the power of practical intellect and well-tuned judgment, forewarned. But the doctor overlooks the power of joy. He discounts the power of art, however artfully proposed. He is blind to the power of beauty—his daughter's newly felt glory. He strips the commonplace child of the magnetically interesting husband she might have had—and what if Morris were made rich by the marriage, what is that to Catherine? And if rich and at ease, would he not be likely to remain kind? Might he not go on inventing her into something spirited and bold? The father, vindictive and dry, relegates the daughter's heart to barrenness and an absent future. He dooms her to a semblance of widowhood—to a mourning as empty as his own. Henceforth, unloved, bereft, unaccommodated, confined to her small domestic parlor, she will become a small domestic Lear. A Lear made mute by smallness.

Who—or what—is to blame? Is it Mrs. Penniman, who by a thousand blandishments has encouraged Morris to believe that a softly importuning Catherine might prevail over her father's hard will? Is it the cavernous greed of an intransigent Morris, whose charms wear off as the money recedes? Is it Dr. Sloper, who places deadly prognostication over hope, and punishment over possibility? Is it Catherine herself, obstinate in her perilous trust? Is it the treacherous idea of the romance of art?

Or perhaps the fault lies in a different breed of art—not the seductions of a transfiguring imagination, but the far darker art of imposture. A harsh and relentless father impersonates a loving and protective parent; a fortune hunter impersonates a sincere lover; a flibbertigibbet aunt impersonates a reliable confidante. And Catherine, when Morris returns after years away, older but no better than before—Catherine for a few deceptive moments appears to him to be the passively quiescent Catherine he remembers. But this too is an imposture. She is fierce; she is strong; she is implacable. Her father is dead, she is rich and unmarried, and Morris, prompted yet again by Mrs. Penniman, once more comes a-courting. Long ago he had reinvented Catherine by pledging her joy. In the wake of abandonment she has reinvented herself—in her father's remorseless image. With quick cruelty she dispatches her belated suitor: the jilter jilted.

But climax is anticlimax. There is no satisfaction in it. *Washington Square* is a novel about the abuse of imagination, the abuse of trust, the abuse of propriety and form; about, above all, the absence of pity. When James spoke of those "manners, customs, usages, habits, forms, upon . . . [which] a novelist lives," he was not unaware that it is on their rupture that a novelist can also—and still more vividly—live. Though it may be a bad thing to break the rules of a fixed society (disinheritance of a child is such a breach, jilting is such a breach), it is a worse thing to break a heart. Whether Dr. Sloper or Morris Townsend is the deeper miscreant is, in the end, a tossup. Is it always right to be right?

Will a wrong motive always do harm? And what are we to think of the secret susceptibilities of the novelist who sets this tale of tragic desertion in the weedy-smelling ailanthus streets of his own childhood, and in the country he himself deserted? "Morris, Morris, you must never despise me!" Catherine is made to cry. Can it be that this is what Henry James heard America whisper in his ear—that he must never despise what he had abandoned?

Shadowy complexities like these aside, *Washington Square* is among James's most exquisitely proportioned shorter masterpieces. "There is no living novelist," Virginia Woolf wrote in 1905, "whose standard is higher, or whose achievement is so consistently great." Her single reservation (she was reviewing *The Golden Bowl*, a work of James's "late style") attached to what she called his "overburdened sentences," "trivial instances of detail which, perpetually insisted on, fatigue without adding to the picture. Genius would have dissolved them, and whole chapters of the same kind, into a single word."

No such stricture can be applied to *Washington Square* (nor, a century after Woolf's impatient complaint, does anyone any longer doubt James's genius). There is no possibility of reader's fatigue in Catherine Sloper's story. Every line, every paragraph, every chapter, is a fleet-footed light brigade, an engine of irony; and the charged wit of the dialogue is equal to Jane Austen's in another celebrated novel of manners and customs, one similarly concerned with getting a young woman married. *Pride and Prejudice* (its preliminary title was *First Impressions*) is a comedy of thwarted courtship that ends in jubilation. Everyone knows its sparkling opening, a sentence incised in literary history, signaling bright vitality: "It is a truth universally acknowledged, that a single man in possession of a good fortune must be in want of a wife." But (given custom and habit) reverse the sexes—and choose the earlier title—and the brilliantly lit comedy is gone; you have Catherine and Morris. The final note of *Washington Square*, a kind of codicil, is dour and dire and unforgettable. It too has left its lasting signal—that of a light growing dimmer: "Catherine, meanwhile, in the parlor, picking up her morsel of fancywork, had seated herself with it again—for life, as it were." The muted fading of that "as it were"—a nuanced gesture typical of James—stands for the snuffing of the light. Even a small and unsung Lear may be consigned to darkness.

Smoke and Fire:
Sylvia Plath's Journals

Sylvia plath's voice, reading her poems on tape, is a daunting, not to say intimidating, astonishment. It is not, as you would expect so many decades after her death, ghostly, a vaporish backwash; it is instead a voice made of marble, the diction burnished, precise, almost inhumanly perfected: as if Eliot's tones, so pervasive in that period, had, with all the authority of their ritualized cadences, been transfused into a woman's veins. The voice is dark and deep and dangerous, the sound not of youth but of some overripe being, an old woman, or even an old man; its register is surprisingly low and nearly sinister; it surprises and unsettles.

It surprises and unsettles, I think, because its hard marble has so long been masked by Styrofoam. Sylvia Plath's posthumous celebrity—her legend—has pitched her into a protean plastic weightlessness. She has become all things to all men, and especially to all women. She has been undone not so much by her own hand as by that deadening thing we nowadays call Icon. Through the throngs of her ideological explicators her voice comes to us as light, high, fragile, and faint. Her grief pales to grievance. "Does not my heat astound you," she asks, accompanied by no question mark, in "Fever 103." But her heat has been purloined by publicity. She is the object of confusion and misunderstanding and mistake.

The mistake is this: that a poet's life weighs in the same scale as the poems themselves. It goes without saying that Sylvia Plath's published journals are archivally valuable, and that they do far more than simply feed our curiosity. In addition to personal revelations—uninhibited news from the inside, so to speak: "Do you realize the illicit sensuous delight that I get from picking my nose? . . . There are so many subtle variations of sensation . . . A delicate, pointed-nailed fifth finger can catch under dry scabs and flakes of mucus in the nostril and draw them out to be looked at . . . God, what a sexual satisfaction!"—in addition to Ancient-Mariner-creatures-of-the-sea moments like these, the journals render the temper of a time, its social and intellectual airs. And here we can discover the abyss between the life and the work, between Plath's days, which are evanescent, and Plath's poems, which are indelible. To look for the poems in the life—in the sense of cause-and-effect—is not merely a tedium; it is a fool's errand.

"The true writer," says Cyril Connolly (who, like most writers, never wrote a masterpiece), "has only one function: to write a masterpiece. Anything less, any partial appeal, marks that writer as bogus." But readers, too, can be bogus. To mine the journals for Plath's despairs and exhilarations, or for her accounts of dresses and boyfriends and dinners—"chicken soup, good and creamy, delicious stuffed tomatoes, turkey with the usual unredeemed chip potatoes and overcooked dried peas"; or to read the journals backward from Plath's suicide in the hope of finding clues to it—all this is bogus. Finally the legend is smoke. Finally there are the poems and only the poems.

Which is not to discount the interest of the times—particularly because Plath defied them, strangely, by not always living up to them. Her youth—an inept word, since she never had anything else—was lived out in a period of rigid hierarchy: it was high art or nothing. Or, rather, it was high art or infinite scorn. The mixture, or side-by-sideness, of high and low, which we take for granted today (whether or not we call it postmodernism), was then inconceivable. Noses were for looking down at. A young writer of verse or prose would no more have thought of entering a contest for *Seventeen* magazine, or dreamed of having stories published in *McCall's* or the *Ladies' Home Journal*, than of sitting down in a lake of muck. The periodicals that serious young writers aspired to were the prestigious so-called "little" magazines, *Partisan* and *Kenyon* and *Hudson*, and a handful of other mystically highbrow quarterlies.

I remember the sensation, in those long-ago days, of opening *The New Yorker* and searching for the poems, and coming nearly simultaneously on two startling poets, Sylvia Plath and Adrienne Cecile Rich (as she then styled herself)—and knowing instantly that there on the page, flaming through it, was, in Plath's words, "pure acetylene." The journals disclose that Plath targeted Rich as her chief rival, soon to be overtaken: "Jealous one am I, green-eyed, spite-seething." On April 17, 1958, at twenty-six, she wrote: "I have the joyous feeling of leashed power—also the feeling that in a year or two I should be 'recognized'—as I am not at all now, though I sit on poems richer than any Adrienne Cecile Rich." Those early poems of Plath's were stitched in gaudy language and technique, secret rhymes intended only for the eye, images bewitched by the neighbor-images they were compelled to serve, each single word rinsed in newness.

And in this same season Plath was longing for what seems incongruous now, and in the rarefied mental scene of fifty-odd years ago was even more incongruous. Virginia Woolf's diaries rest easily alongside the body of her other writing; they are an equal masterwork. Artistically, they are all at high tide. Sylvia Plath's journals are not; they are jagged things. Plath wanted to succeed in the slick women's magazines and in the *Saturday Evening Post*. The stories were sent there; the poems went to *The New Yorker*, the *Atlantic*, and *Harper's Magazine*. She read Melville and James and Yeats and of course Eliot; and meanwhile she was swallowing the *Ladies' Home Journal* whole, setting down long paragraphs recounting the plots of its published stories, and listing inventories of possible plots of her own: "Husband comes home; new understanding . . . beautiful cakes." She imagined being "a vagabond wife," yet she rejoiced in a husband who was, she crowed, "the man the unsatisfied ladies scan the *Ladies' Home Journal* for, the man women read romantic novels for . . . and I love cooking for him (made him a lemon layer cake last night) and being secretary, and all."

She was not a bluestocking or a half-bohemian like the rest of the strenuous literary strivers of the same generation. She never went down to the Village to gawk at Auden shuffling along in his carpet slippers, or to catch a glimpse of Marianne Moore in her tricorn hat. Instead she sailed up to *Mademoiselle* as a fashion-magazine prizewinner and interviewed Marianne Moore as her prize, wearing a double string of pearls and a flat little hat of her own over a polished every-hair-in-place pageboy. She was both Emily Dickinson and Betty Crocker—which is why the journals are inscrutable, and in this respect more shocking than the suicide.

The journals: the gifted drawings, the passages of lyrical narrative, the cutting and cunning intellect, the jealousy, the anger, the lemon layer cakes, the slicks, the clear ascent from girlish infatuations to sober maturity, the whole human spectrum—and then the effectively superhuman, the year-by-year accretion of the journals themselves; and the drive, the drive, the drive. But come back to the *Collected Poems*—the full fierce force of their conflagrations—and the journals and their lemon cakes and their good husband and their bad husband, all taken together, become as ash. "Does not my heat astound you," she asks, and yes, it burns all the rest to dross.

KIPLING:
A POSTCOLONIAL
FOOTNOTE

RUDYARD KIPLING IS INCONTROVERTIBLY one of the most renowned writers of the early twentieth century. Yet despite his name's irrepressible familiarity, he is also among the most disavowed. There may still be imaginatively wise children who prefer the enchantments of any page of *Just So Stories* (adorned with Kipling's own magical illustrations and ingenious verses) to the crude smatterings of the film cartoons—but Kipling is vastly more than a children's treasure. All the same, serious readers long ago relinquished him: who now speaks of Kipling?

The reason is partly contemporary political condemnation —enlightened postcolonial disdain—and partly contemporary literary prejudice. Together with Conrad, Kipling carries the opprobrium of empire, "the white man's burden," though his lavish Indian stories are often sympathetically and vividly understanding of both Hindu and Muslim. And he is ignored on the literary side because in the period of Joyce's blooming Kipling's prose declined to be tricked out with the obvious involutions of modernism. Unlike Joyce, James, and Woolf, he gets at the interiors of his characters by boring inward from the rind. Yet he writes the most inventive, the most idiosyncratic, the most scrupulously surreal English sentences of his century (next to which Woolf's are more predictably commonplace).

Kipling's late stories (he died in 1937) — "The Wish House" (in virtuoso dialect), "Dayspring Mishandled," "Mary Postgate," "The Gardener," "The Eye of Allah," "Baa Baa Black Sheep" (an autobiographical revelation), "Mrs. Bathhurst," and so many others — form a compact body of some of the strongest fiction of the last hundred years: sly, penetrating, ironically turned. Kipling's wizardry for setting language on its ear, his insight into every variety of humanity, his zest for science, for ghosts, for crowds, for countryside, cast him as a master of kaleidoscopic narrative; no strand of civilization escapes his worldly genius. So even the most zealous proponents of postcolonial theory deserve — or at least ought not to eschew — the pleasurable rewards of Kipling.

DELMORE SCHWARTZ:
THE WILLED ABORTION
OF THE SELF

§ LIKE SYLVIA PLATH a generation later, like Shelley a century before, Delmore Schwartz is one of those poets whose life inescapably rivals the work. Plath's fame is linked as much to the shock of the suicide as to the shock of the poetry; the wild romance of Shelley's lines is fulfilled in the drama of the drowning. And Delmore Schwartz catapults past the fickleness of mere reputation into something close to legend. What puts him there is not his ignominious end—he died, at fifty-three, in chaotic solitude in a Manhattan hotel—but the clamorous periods of derangement that rocked him, side by side with spurts of virtuosity. It was a catastrophic life—turbulent, demanding, importuning, drinking, pill-swallowing, competitive, suspicious, litigious. He reveled in celebrity when it came to him and abused the friendships it attracted. At one point he appeared ready to sue nearly every literary luminary he knew. His incessant talk turned to aggressive harangue and accusation. But he early saw into the logic of his madness, attributing it to the rage of an ambition too overreaching ever to be attained. "The torment of disappointed hope becomes a brutality to myself," he wrote.

He was, like many of the so-called New York Intellectuals of his generation, the aspiring son of Jewish immigrants. His parents were mismatched; his philandering father prospered in real estate until the Crash. Delmore followed sports, went obsessively to the movies, and judged his family and broken household with a harshly dismissive yet hotly bonded eye. As an undergraduate at the University of Wisconsin, he fell deliriously into modernism, Eliot and Pound and Joyce, and was steeped in avant-garde periodicals like *Hound & Horn*—but he failed Latin, and except for English made an indifferent record. He returned to New York to study philosophy with Sidney Hook and James Burnham at NYU's Washington Square College, where he met the first of his two wives. Both eventually left him; upheaval and rancor trailed him all his fabled days.

Philosophy next lured him to Harvard. He worked at it under the eminent Alfred North Whitehead, but at length began to waver, and poetry won out. Yet philosophy infiltrated the poetry —not through narrow cognitive distinctions, but through discerning the naked *thereness* of things. Philosophy gave his lines the crystalline quality of naiveté: the peculiar power to gaze into the self, or the world, as objects never before seen or contemplated. He became a metaphysician of the near-at-hand:

> If you look long enough at anything
> It will become extremely interesting;
> If you look very long at anything
> It will become rich, manifold, fascinating.

Out of Whitehead's "the withness of the body" came

> The heavy bear who goes with me,
> A manifold honey to smear his face,
> Clumsy and lumbering here and there,
> The central ton of every place
>
> . . .

That inescapable animal that walks with me,
Has followed me since the black womb held,
Moves where I move, distorting my gesture,
A caricature, a swollen shadow,
A stupid clown of the spirit's motive,
Perplexes and affronts with his own darkness,
The secret life of belly and bone,
Opaque, too near, my private, yet unknown . . .

The penetration of this opacity Schwartz called "the parsing of context." His own body was a context to be parsed, however mercilessly, and even his name, the lyrical Delmore, was an outerness hinting at inner life: on the principle of *nomen est numen*— name is spirit—only a poet could be destined for so poetic a name. But such parsing will not inevitably lead to self-understanding. In "March 29" he cries:

Behold! For we are absent from our knowledge, we are
lost to the common undertaking of our lives, there are
unleashed within us the small animals of silence. . . .

And in the shimmeringly titled "In the Naked Bed, in Plato's Cave" an alert heaping up of the poet's surround accretes—aural, visual, atmospheric, above all needlingly concrete: the window and the window curtains, trucks passing, the milkman's footsteps, the bottles' clink, the horse, the street, the streetlight, the sky, a car's starter, a chair, a mirror, a dresser, a wall, a birdcall! Though each of these is possessed by an explicit presence, taken together all fall into elusive enigma:

Perplexed, still wet
With sleep, affectionate, hungry and cold. So, so,
O son of man, the ignorant night, the travail

Of early morning, the mystery of beginning
Again and again,

> while History is unforgiven.

From the bedroom and its furnishings, to the mundane city-sounds of early morning, to the heartless chronicle of humankind.

Why is history unforgiven? Perhaps because it is, after all, history, out of which all contradictions can be wrested and made palpable. "I hate an abstract thing," he complains in "The Ballad of the Children of the Czar"—wherein the czar's children bounce a ball in the czar's garden, while that same year Delmore, "aged two, irrational," eats a baked potato in Brooklyn, "six thousand miles apart." The czar's children play among flowerbeds, but the poet recalls that his grandfather, coughing and wretched in the czar's army, flees to America, "to become," he notes sardonically, "a king himself." The bouncing ball among the flowers and the baked potato in Brooklyn swell hugely, balefully, transmuted finally into the round earth itself, the "wheeling, whirling world":

A pitiless, purposeless Thing,
Arbitrary and unspent

. . .

I am overtaken by terror
Thinking of my father's fathers,
And of my own will.

The innocently small, the innocently tangible, can shockingly lurch into widening empty blind unknowingness: so that elsewhere, a night train with its passengers, the smoke, the dark, the "pencil lines of telephone posts, crucified," the scenes that rush by, turning away from hope, from history itself, reveal only "the overnight endless trip to the famous unfathomable abyss":

> O your life, your lonely life
> What have you done with it,
> And done with the great gift of consciousness?

Writing of Baudelaire, and purporting to enact the French poet's recklessly desperate psyche, it is himself whom Schwartz uncovers:

> I am sick of this life of furnished rooms.
> I am sick of having colds and headaches:
> You know my strange life. Every day brings
>
> Its quota of wrath. You little know
> A poet's life, dear Mother: I must write poems,
> The most fatiguing of occupations.

Though intimations of the then prevailing imperium of *The Waste Land* seep through many of Schwartz's verses, and though they are permeated by the sort of acutely objective self-consciousness that characterizes much of the modernist ethos, Schwartz cannot, in either his poetry or his prose, be wholly defined as a modernist—a judgment that might have alarmed him. The tenor of his mind is largely like the tenor of his extravagantly Romantic given name—Romantically excessive, even incongruous, especially in the company of workaday Schwartz. Allusions, nineteenth-century-style, to Dionysus and Venus, to "Attic dust," "love's victory," "the day's splendor," "lights' glory," "his smile which glows like that of the spring moon," "the miracle of love," and abundantly more in that vein, attest more to Keats than to Prufrock, and more to earnest odes to beauty and despair than to anxious deadpan skeptical modernist reticence. "Everywhere radiance glows like a garden in stillness blossoming" is an idiom that, in all its shameless loveliness, seizes on the old roots of poetry. And here, in "Seurat's Sunday Afternoon along the Seine," one can catch, with rapt directness, the unconcealed Keatsian tone:

> O happy, happy throng,
> It is forever Sunday, summer, free

All this discloses a poet's escape, if he wills it, from the commanding Zeitgeist. Or even if he does not will it, if it comes unwittingly, unsummoned, from his nature—libertarian, untethered, deaf to all authority but the imperative inward chant. How else account for the startling grandeur of "Starlight Like Intuition Pierced the Twelve," a title that, even apart from the lines that follow, carries a nimbus almost too bright to bear?

Put it that the poetry is Delmore; its themes are chiefly (and in his own fearsome words) awe and abyss. But the prose? The prose is Schwartz. The language of the stories is plain, simple, never convoluted or mandarin; practical and ordinary. "It is Sunday afternoon, June 12th, 1909, and my father is on his way to visit my mother," commences the second paragraph of "In Dreams Begin Responsibilities," Schwartz's most celebrated fiction. No Seurat's Sunday afternoon here; no happy throngs. The narrator sits in a darkened movie house in the days of silent film, witnessing the unfolding courtship of his parents. "The shots themselves," he explains, "are full of dots and rays, as if it were raining when the picture was photographed. The light is bad." And in the narrative itself there are few rays and many dots: the sentences are short and declarative:

> As my father enters, my grandfather rises from the table and shakes hands with him. My mother has run upstairs to tidy

herself. My grandmother asks my father if he has had dinner, and tells him that Rose will be downstairs soon. My grandfather opens the conversation by remarking on the mild June weather. My father sits uncomfortably near the table, holding his hat in his hand. My grandmother tells my aunt to take my father's hat.

These flat, even commonplace, cadences—as flat and commonplace as the name Schwartz—appear to have no affinity with the baroque Delmorean movements of the poems. Did the same mind coin them? At first sight, hardly; the gap between verse and fiction seems antagonistic, nearly schizophrenic: on the one hand wild eloquence (the wine pitcher broken and spilling), while on the other subdued dry orderliness. Yet the stories have a labyrinthine undersea quality; cumulatively, the pedestrian turns tragic and surreal. As the narrator sees his father proposing marriage to his mother on the movie screen, he leaps out of his seat and shouts, "Don't do it. It's not too late to change your minds, both of you. Nothing good will come of it, only remorse, hatred, scandal, and two children whose characters are monstrous." What has begun prosaically becomes hideously visionary: the Delmorean abyss again opening, ready to swallow the dreamer; the dreamer's prefigured and ineluctable birth dreaded and doomed. It is a terrifying tale of the willed abortion of the self.

Movies—the dream palaces of the thirties and forties—dominate other fictions. "Screeno" recalls a period when theaters featured on-stage allurements in addition to the picture, often in the form of lotteries offering money prizes. Cornelius Schmidt, a lonely and impoverished self-declared young poet, wins at Screeno, at first resenting and then championing a usurping rival for the prize. The story pivots on the shiftings of perception and reality, on the longings of youth and the lamentations of age; and on uncanny Kafkan reversals. Here and there philosophy peers in: "'Oh,' said Cornelius to himself, 'they are going to start the whole objective and subjective business again'"—until it is finally clear that this story, too, owes more to the shadows of dreams than to local movie-house history. The moviegoer with the winning ticket is gambling for control of his slippery life—below which, as always, gapes the abyss.

A third movie story concerns Hugo Bauer, a rich financier who lusts after a Hollywood screen goddess, whom he ultimately marries. Divorce quickly follows. But it is her naked image he has fallen in love with, the seductive phantom projected in her notorious film, *The Heights of Joy*. To possess this image wholly for himself, he attempts to buy and destroy all existing copies of it, "devoting himself to a senseless quest in which his life became just as bewitched and monomaniacal, as passionate and as narrow, as the life of a gambler or a lyric poet." Despite every effort, the film cannot be sequestered from other eyes, since new copies can repeatedly be made; but years later, when the marriage is long forgotten, the image of Hugo Bauer's former wife, "naked and radiant as the moonlight on a midsummer night, shining and distant and unattainable," unreels before him, and he is exalted.

The stories are all of a piece. They are shrewd Schwartzian tricksters that may momentarily fool you into thinking you have been kidnapped into the land of the declarative sentence; but this is sleight of hand. In the end the stories are seen to be, bone for bone, blood for blood, of the same Delmorean germ plasm as the poems. A case in point is "The Statues," a vision in which a strange snow falls, assuming permanent forms that will not melt or give way.

> Many of these statues were grotesque. Some were monstrous. Some resembled human figures, and although they were of a

perfect verisimilitude in all else, the faces were at times blank as a plate, distorted like gargoyles, or obscene, as when, in certain suburbs, figures clung to each other in an embrace which was hardly ambiguous. Elsewhere, however, the statues had the rotundity and the plumpness of the cumulus clouds of a summer's day, the solidity and the stillness of fine buildings, or the pure and easy design of some flowers. Everywhere were forms which delighted the eye either as fresh complexes of previously known designs, or compositions which seemed to exhaust the possibility of arrangement.

The stories, like many of the poems, are dreams without responsibilities. They are their own cause, their own authority, their own unreasoning reason.

§

Delmore Schwartz, some dare to say, is in eclipse. With the acceleration of the generations, his fame is long dimmed; the wunderkind he once was is unremembered. His life—that tumultuous unstoppable speechifying, the madness that tossed and tormented and ruined him—stands like one of those impermeable statues of his imagining. In a 1966 letter to Elizabeth Bishop, Robert Lowell, himself not unfamiliar with seizures of madness, described Schwartz in his last days as "a sluggish, sometimes angry spider—no hurry, no motion, Delmore's voice, almost inaudible, dead, intuitive, pointing somewhere, then the strings tightening, the roar of rage—too much, too much for us!" And finally, Saul Bellow, in snatching Schwartz's persona for *Humboldt's Gift*, knowingly wrote his epitaph:

For after all Humboldt did what poets in crass America are supposed to do. He chased ruin and death even harder than he had chased women. He blew his talent and his health and reached home, the grave, in a dusty slide. He plowed himself under. . . . Such was the attitude reflected in the picture of Humboldt the *Times* chose to use. It was one of those mad-rotten-majesty pictures—spooky, humorless, glaring furiously with tight lips, mumpish or scrofulous cheeks, a scarred forehead, and a look of enraged, ravaged childishness. This was the Humboldt of conspiracies, putsches, accusations, tantrums, the Bellevue Hospital Humboldt.

But a poet all the same. He plowed himself under? Never mind. Delmore Schwartz in death casts off the heavy bear, leaving behind awe and abyss, dream and chant.

Lionel Trilling
and the Buried Life

§ Half a century ago, Lionel Trilling summoned me into his office at Columbia University to be interviewed for admission to his renowned graduate seminar. For ten minutes or so I sat fixed under his gray prosecutorial eye; he seemed gray all over—his suit, his tie, the level line of his hair, his nostrils with their monarchical arches. His manner was reticent, hiddenly mocking, almost inviolable. I saw him as a kind of monument, and I hoped for access to his seminar less for the sake of what I would study there than for proximity to his fame. It was the Age of Criticism—the marmoreal tag given to it by Randall Jarrell, one of its poet-critics—and Trilling was its most eminent literary intellectual. *The Liberal Imagination*, his landmark work—a collection of sixteen essays previously published mainly in literary quarterlies—had appeared only the year before, in 1950; it had catapulted an already vigorous reputation into something hierarchical: rank, influence, authority.

From the 1940s on, the Age of Criticism had been especially fruitful, and had multiplied so many literary exegetes and ruminators that, with all their differences, they had come to constitute an establishment. They might call themselves Southern Agrarians, like Allen Tate and John Crowe Ransom, or Neo-Thomists, like

Eliseo Vivas, or formalists, like Cleanth Brooks—but whatever the rubric and whatever the tendency, the mantle of New Criticism fell over all of them. Their essays had a formidable resonance in the literature departments of universities in both England and America, though nowhere so impressively as in the American academy. Nowadays the jingling mantra of their illustrious names—I. A. Richards, William Empson (whose *Seven Types of Ambiguity* was once reigning doctrine), René Wellek, W. K. Wimsatt, Kenneth Burke, Yvor Winters—is a faded archaism, together with the monastic tenets of New Criticism itself. In its ascendancy the chief dogma of New Criticism, irresistible and indisputable, was *explication de texte*, or close reading, which meant the exclusion of all external interpretive biases: no politics, no past, no social forms, no ethics. Instead, the isolated purity of metaphor, image, "tension," irony—absolutist elements that were said to be objectively inherent in the work, which was looked on as a self-enclosed artifact. In the most up-to-date graduate schools of the time (I was fresh from one of these), all this was felt not as a literary movement, but as a theology linked to eternity. It was with such a credo—New Criticism as sacrosanct truth—that I arrived at Trilling's office door.

His ridicule, courteous and restrained, was direct enough. "You don't really believe," he asked—it was accusation rather than question—"that literature has nothing to do with psychology, with biography or society or history?" I did believe it; I had been trained to believe it. Who of my generation was not susceptible to that aesthetic casuistry? But it was instantly plain that to admit to adherence to New Critical precepts would shut me out from the seminar; so, just as instantly, I switched allegiance to the other side, though five minutes before I had scarcely known that there was another side. It was the seminar I coveted—not the substance of the seminar (Victorian social theorists), but some unfathomable emanation of the mind that presided over it. I wanted to witness the enigma of fame.

The seminar turned out to be a disappointment. In one respect it confirmed everything Trilling had heralded in those electrifying ten minutes in his office: it was saturated in social and historical issues. New Criticism had no status here and was altogether shunned; after all, Trilling in *The Liberal Imagination* had assailed what he called the New Critics' pervasive "anxiety lest the work of art be other than totally self-contained." In this self-contained room of ambitious young scholars—headed almost universally for academic careers—there were more personal anxieties. Trilling was disconsolate and irritable. He was impatient; often he seemed fatigued. He had one or two favorites, whom he would praise profusely—but he was sarcastic or indifferent to others. If a comment struck him as inadequate, his lanternlike eyes would silence the speaker with barely disguised dismissal; his gray back was a wall of contempt, of wishing to be elsewhere.

Trilling did wish to be elsewhere, and had already taken steps to effect it. While the semester was running its course, and I sat cowed and bewildered by fame's unexpected face, he was setting down in his private notebooks an account of his disgust for the seminar and his relief in his coming release from it. The seminar, he wrote,

> needs a total intellectual and emotional involvement that I shld never want to make. . . . And then the students dismay me . . . But then all graduate students trouble & in a way repel me and I must put down here the sensation of liberation I experienced when I arranged for my withdrawal from the graduate school, from seminars. . . . For one thing I became a

public character and always on view, having to live up to the demands made upon a public character, & finding that the role seemed to grow inward. . . . And here I should set down my ever-growing dislike of teaching & the systematic study of literature more and more it goes against the grain.

These extraordinary thoughts were recorded in 1951. Trilling would continue to teach for the next quarter century, until his death in 1975, and his position as "public character" would grow in prominence and distinction. But eleven years later, in 1962, after confessing his admiration for a novel by Sartre, he was lamenting (again in the seclusion of his notebooks), "Nothing has so filled me with shame and regret at what I have not done." A hollow introspection, secretly whispered while standing in the very palm of literary fame. ("I hear on all sides," he had written some years earlier, "of the extent of my reputation—which some call 'fame.' . . . It is the thing I have wanted from childhood on—although of course in much greater degree.") By 1962, Trilling had published a major work on Matthew Arnold, a vanguard study of E. M. Forster, and more than fifty consummately original essays collected in three highly influential volumes. He had also written a novel. He was, by any standard, a "figure," and by his own standard especially. Assessing George Orwell—"He is not merely a writer, he is a figure"—he attached this term to those who "are what they write, whom we think of as standing for something as men because of what they have written in their books. They preside, as it were, over certain ideas and attitudes."

Trilling's ideas, particularly his political ideas, evolved from decade to decade, but his attitudes remained consistent. He stood for—he presided over—a disposition toward the claims of morality. "My own interests," he said in a 1961 essay on teaching, "lead me to see literary situations as cultural situations, and cultural situations as great elaborate fights about moral issues, and moral issues as having something to do with gratuitously chosen images of personal being, and images of personal being as having something to do with literary style." This was unmistakably the portrait of a figure, the man who is what he writes; the tone is a public one of self-knowledge and confidence. Yet in July of that same year Trilling was privately regretting what he had made of his life, and grieving that he was not someone else:

> —Death of Ernest Hemingway. . . .—who would suppose how much he has haunted me? How much he existed in my mind—as a reproach? He was the only writer of our time I envied. I respected him in his most foolish postures and in his worst work.

Haunted by Hemingway? Envy? Reproach? Trilling was fifty-six when he sequestered these emotions in his notebooks. But in 1933, at twenty-eight, his Columbia position still provisional and no permanent appointment in sight, he was reproaching himself still more vehemently.

> Saw a letter Hemingway wrote to Kip [Clifton Fadiman]—a crazy letter, written when he was drunk—self-revealing, arrogant, scared, trivial, absurd; yet felt from reading it how right such a man is compared to the "good minds" of my university life—how he will produce and mean something to the world . . . how his life which he could expose without dignity and which is anarchic and "childish" is a better life than anyone I know could live, and right for his job. And how far-far-far I am going from being a writer—how less and less I have the material and the mind and the will. A few—very few—more years and the last chance will be gone.

The surprisingly incongruous attraction to Hemingway, the envy, the reproach, the regret, the dark intimations of something irretrievable: none of this moodiness was visible in the public character. That Trilling—the incarnation of dignity, discipline, moderation—should look wistfully to the heedlessness and anarchy he saw in Hemingway is on the face of it unimaginable. In the corpus of the masterful essays this underground desire to shed or oppose civilization can be glimpsed only once or twice, and then mainly through peepholes in the prose. Writing of the stories in Isaac Babel's *Red Cavalry* (a Jew riding with the Red Army's Cossacks), Trilling exposed the skeleton of his internal antithesis: "The Jew conceived his own ideal character to consist in his being intellectual, pacific, humane. The Cossack was physical, violent, without mind or manners." By inheritance and temperament, Trilling was the first. He understood the writer (by which he meant the novelist) to be a type radically different from himself: instinctual, a reckless darer, a hero. Paraphrasing Henry James, he agreed that "the artist quite as much as any man of action carries his ultimate commitment and his death warrant in his pocket." As a teacher of literature, as the kind of honored public character he had become, he was immured in the intellectual, the pacific, the humane; there was no risk, no death warrant, in the reflective life of the literary essayist. Musing harshly on his Columbia colleagues, he deplored "such people as Mark VD [Van Doren], who yearly seems to me to grow weaker and weaker, more academic, less a person." As for Trilling himself: "My being a professor and a much respected and even admired one is a great hoax. . . . Suppose I were to dare to believe that one could be a professor and a man! and a writer!" Here was bitterness, here was regret: he did not believe that a professor could be truly a man; only the writer, with his ultimate commitment to the wilderness of the imagination, was truly a man.

In approaching such ironies—Trilling as self-repudiator, Trilling as failed writer—one ought to be warned. Journal entries, those vessels of discontent, are notoriously fickle, subject to the torque of mutable feeling, while power flourishes elsewhere. Even if a thread of constancy appears to run through years of an interior record, it is useful to be tentative. Without caution, speculation falls into usurpation. Though the living Trilling was valued and acclaimed, the dead Trilling has been made into a puppet, violated by at least two memoirists: his wife and his son. Diana Trilling, in her 1993 account of their marriage, insisted that she taught him how to write. "He had been writing and publishing for some years before we met," she admitted, "but I helped him to write more attractively, with more clarity and rigor both of thought and expression. His prose had hitherto tended to laxness. Itself not disciplined, it could allow for undisciplined thinking. . . . I was relentless in my editorial address to every word he wrote." If this seems unlikely—and more than that, injurious —James Trilling's claim (in a polemic in the *American Scholar*) that his father suffered from attention deficit disorder is still more troubling. Diana Trilling names herself the bestower of style. James Trilling presumes to account for the properties of that style. By insinuating weakness where there was sovereignty, both tend to undermine Trilling's public standing from a private vantage. Inevitably, the malicious dust of a colossus pulled down fills the nostrils.

Trilling's capacious prose was complex and scrupulous. It qualified, weighed, probed; it was the opposite of lax, merging taut lines of thought from disparate starting points. It was a manner that had been moved to fine discriminations ever since, at twenty-one, Trilling began to write for the *Menorah Journal*, a Jewish literary and cultural periodical edited by Elliot Cohen (who later founded *Commentary*). Years afterward, Trilling wrote lovingly of Cohen as "the only great teacher I have ever had," a man who owned "the unremitting passion of genius." With Cohen's encouragement (and Cohen was himself still in his twenties), Trilling reviewed novels by such contemporary luminaries as Ludwig Lewisohn, Robert Nathan, and Lion Feuchtwanger, poetry by Charles Reznikoff and Louis Untermeyer ("Mr. Untermeyer is not a good poet, American or Jewish"), and translations from the Yiddish. He published essays both historical and speculative, ranging from "A Friend of Byron" to "The Changing Myth of the Jew," and though over the decades his style grew more elaborately nuanced, its distinction, and the reach and versatility that defined it, was brilliantly evident from the first. His colleagues on the magazine included Clifton Fadiman, Lewis Mumford, Charles Beard, and Mark Van Doren—essayists all; but Trilling had a more crucial ambition. The *Menorah Journal* became the depository of story after story; he wrote more short fiction now than at any other time in his life. His last labor of fiction was quietly consummated in 1947, when he was forty-two, with the publication of *The Middle of the Journey*, his only novel— and from the point of view of the academy, where he seemed so much at home, it came unexpectedly.

Yet all along, confessional sighs of loss and competitiveness had been turning up in the notebooks: "Story of a university teacher who never got to write"—an idea for a story that never got written. After a visit from Allen Ginsberg, a former student: "We spoke of Kerouac's book. I predicted that it would not be good & insisted. But later I saw with what bitterness I had made the prediction—not wanting K's book to be good." These are the ruminations not of a teacher or a critic, but of a writer of fiction desperate to be in the running. "The attack on my novel," he recorded, "that it is gray, bloodless, intellectual, without passion, is always made with great personal feeling, with anger.—How dared I presume?"

He did not presume again. There were no other novels. By 1945 the stories, and the ideas for stories, had trickled to a stop. That stricken cry of his middle age, mourning the death of Hemingway, was also a lamentation for the death of another novelist —himself.

In his study of Matthew Arnold—a majestic work begun at twenty-three and submitted as his doctoral dissertation a decade later—Trilling spoke of a "feeling of intimacy" with his subject. The attachment was lifelong. He described Arnold's style as "subtle critical dialectic" and his method as requiring "that we suspend our absolute standards and look at events and ideas, past or present, in the light of their historical determinants." These Arnoldian leitmotifs became Trilling's own critical instruments, reflecting the veiled melancholia and austerity of Arnold's famed "high seriousness." But there was something else the young Trilling took from Arnold—a strangely predictive force embedded in a single poem. Twice in the course of his biography of a mind, as he called it, Trilling quotes phrases—the same phrases —from "The Buried Life," Arnold's dejected stanzas on the diminution of his poetic stream:

> And we have been on many thousand lines,
> And we have shown, on each, spirit and power,
> But hardly have we, for one little hour,
> Been on our own line, have we been ourselves.
> . . .
> And long we try in vain to speak and act
> Our hidden self, and what we say and do
> Is eloquent, is well—but 'tis not true!

"The Muse has gone away," Trilling comments. "Men feel, as they leave youth, that they have more or less consciously assumed a role by excluding some of the once-present elements from themselves. But ever after they are haunted by the fear that they might have selected another, better, role, that perhaps they have made the wrong choice." Even as Trilling was penning these relentless words, he was howling in his journal their anguished echo: *how far-far-far I am going from being a writer. . . . A few — very few — more years and the last chance will be gone.* Before he was thirty, he was already seeing Arnold as the prophet of his own buried life. The public character he would acquire, his status as a figure, was eloquent, was well; but the Muse who lights the hidden self had gone away.

§

Since Trilling's death in 1975, the literary culture he espoused and embodied has itself gone away. English departments today harbor few defenders of literary high seriousness as Trilling conceived and felt it. In an unfinished essay truncated by his final illness—"Why We Read Jane Austen"—Trilling set out to explain "the aim of traditional humanistic education." Its purpose, he said, was to read "about the conduct of other people as presented by a writer highly endowed with moral imagination" and "to see this conduct as relevant to [our] own . . . in that it redeems the individual from moral torpor; its communal effect," he concluded, "is often said to be decisive in human existence." He went on to modify and modulate and reconsider, bringing in contradictory examples from history and ethnology, and offering "at least a little complication to humanism's rather simple view of the relation in which our moral lives stood to other cultures"—but the argument against moral torpor held. Twenty years earlier, musing on

Jane Austen's *Mansfield Park*, he had written, "Never before had the moral life been shown as she shows it to be, never before had it been conceived to be so complex and difficult and exhausting," and, shockingly, he announced, "She is the first to be aware of the Terror which rules our moral situation, the ubiquitous anonymous judgment to which we respond. . . . She herself is an agent of the Terror." He said the same of Robert Frost, in a notoriously revisionist speech at a dinner honoring Frost's eighty-fifth birthday.

Almost no one nowadays comes to literary criticism with these premises and intonations. Little of Trilling's intellectual cosmos survives, having been displaced by a perfervid and constantly evanescing succession of rapidly outmoded theoretical movements: structuralism, deconstruction, cultural studies, gender studies, queer studies, postcolonialism. It is Trilling himself who represents the buried life of American literary culture — the brooding body of his essays, their opalescent crisscross of clauses, the minute waverings of his oscilloscopic mind, above all his now nearly incomprehensible influence. His name has dimmed. In the graduate schools his work is mostly unread, and his ideas undiscussed. His ideas were large and cumulative and, knot by knot, unnerving: his method was not to knit up but to unravel. Rather than zero in on a single aspect of human life and examine it as if it were an entire civilization (a current academic tendency), he did the opposite. In the broad imprint of any social period he read something of exigent present need or taste, enacted against the hot concerns of the past, but nearly always with contemporary habits of thought at the forefront. In pondering the place of "duty" in the Victorian novel, for instance, and more generally in the England of the nineteenth century, he set out to counter the cant of the middle of the twentieth:

Such figures as the engineer Daniel Doyce of *Little Dorrit* or Dr. Lydgate of *Middlemarch* represent the developing belief that a man's moral life is bound up with his loyalty to the discipline of his calling. . . . The Church, in its dominant form and characteristic virtue, was here quite at one with the tendency of secular feeling; its preoccupation may be said to have been less with the achievement of salvation than with the performance of duty.

The word grates upon our moral ear. We do what we should do, but we shrink from giving it the name of duty. "Co-operation," "social-mindedness," the "sense of the group," "class solidarity"—these locutions do not mean what duty means. They have been invented precisely for the purpose of describing right conduct in such a way as not to imply what duty implies—a self whose impulses and desires are very strong, and a willingness to subordinate those impulses and desires to the claim of some external nonpersonal good. The new locutions are meant to suggest that right action is typically to be performed without any pain to the self.

The men of the nineteenth century did not imagine this possibility. They thought that morality was terribly hard to achieve, at the cost of renunciation and sacrifice. We of our time often wonder what could have made the difficulty. . . . That the self may destroy the self by the very energies that define its being, that the self may be preserved by the negation of its own energies—this, whether or not we agree, makes a paradox, makes an irony, that catches our imagination. Much of the nineteenth-century preoccupation with duty was not love of law for its own sake, but rather a concern with the hygiene of the self.

"The hygiene of the self": the phrase is Trilling distilled. From the tangled English garden of an intricate foreign culture

—a culture long gone—he plucked the one telling thorn, the thorn most likely to draw blood from the living.

§

"Trilling was our last Victorian sage," Mark Krupnick, author of a book-length consideration of Trilling's career, wrote from the perspective of 1986. It was a judgment designed to suggest not mustiness but something more pressing and expansive: what contemporary critic will speak, directly and repeatedly, as Trilling did, of "the contradictions, paradoxes and dangers of the moral life"? These stringent words appear in the introduction to Trilling's 1943 study of E. M. Forster, where the term "liberal imagination" first crops up. Some time later, in his rebuke to Stalinism in *The Liberal Imagination*, Trilling proposed contradiction and paradox as an antidote to ideology, which he saw as simple, utopian, and authoritarian. "The job of criticism," he insisted, was "to recall liberalism to its first essential imagination of variousness and possibility, which implies the awareness of complexity and difficulty." All this was a response to the pervasive politics of the thirties and forties. Trilling himself had been, briefly, an active radical, a member of the Communist-led National Committee for the Defense of Political Prisoners; he resigned in 1933. Youthful associations of this kind were widespread among intellectuals in that fermenting period of Depression and the rise of fascism in Europe. In Chicago, Saul Bellow and Isaac Rosenfeld were in an identical fever of radical world upheaval. "Politics was everywhere," Rosenfeld recalled, looking back. "One ate and drank it." Trilling was quicker than most to fall away.

But when he advised the liberals of the forties to turn from "agencies, and bureaus, and technicians," and to cultivate instead a "lively sense of contingency and possibility," and when he was troubled by his complacent students of the fifties who glibly ac-

cepted antithetical ideas without resistance or perturbation—
who were, in fact, bored by the subversive and the antisocial—
how could he have foreseen the riotous campus demonstrations
of 1968? In connecting politics with literature—"the politics of
culture," he called it—he was unwittingly entering the vestibule
of the politicization of literature, a commonplace in today's universities. Unwitting or not, Trilling was bemused to see how the
impulse of unrestraint that inflamed the modern masters—Conrad, Mann, Lawrence, Kafka, Nietzsche—was beginning to infiltrate, and finally take over, popular thought and style. These writers, he pointed out, with all their relentless counterminings,
asked "every question that is forbidden in polite society." By the
1970s, no question remained that was forbidden in polite society,
and no answer, either; there was little left of the notion of polite
society altogether. What was liberty for Lawrence became liber-
tinism in the streets. The bold contrariness of the moderns had
succeeded so well that Trilling starchily named its dominance in
the country at large "the adversary culture." Babbitt and H. L.
Mencken's booboisie were routed. Conrad's heart of darkness—
the instinctual storm—that had once been the esoteric province
of modernist high art had gone public. First the professors, then
the rappers; or vice versa. The Cossacks were astride the politics
of culture.

Such were Trilling's ultimate convictions, hidden under the
ornate historical scaffolding of *Sincerity and Authenticity*, the
Charles Eliot Norton Lectures he delivered at Harvard in 1970.
In language grown more and more imbricated, more and more
allergic to self-disclosure, he indicted the empty sentimentality of
"egalitarian hedonism." Outside the lecture hall, the indictment
was muted, and so oblique as to seem equivocal. In 1974, Norman Podhoretz, who headed *Commentary* (where Trilling had

long published), faulted his former teacher for his hesitations and charged him with a failure of nerve in the face of "a resurgence of philistinism, very often of simple cultural barbarism." Trilling's response was that he had been overtaken by fatigue. "One's reaction was likely to be a despairing shrug," he said. On the Vietnam issue he remained unengaged. But hesitation and ambivalence had been in the grain of his literary temperament from the beginning; they lurked in the short stories he wrote in his twenties. He preferred ambiguity to resolution. He was attracted to the indeterminacies of negative capability, Keats's gauzy formula for "remaining content with half-knowledge," "being in uncertainties, mystery, doubts." In essay after essay he alluded to contingency, the conditioned life, the limits of the unavoidable and the unchangeable. Freud's *Civilization and Its Discontents*, with its bleak recognitions, was a touchstone; he came back to it again and again.

§

Probably no literary critic of Trilling's standing, with a history of so enduring and authoritative a presence, is in greater eclipse than Lionel Trilling. Edmund Wilson may no longer be widely read, but he survives as a vivid cultural witness, perhaps because of his connection with the clouds of legend that continue to trail Scott Fitzgerald and Hemingway; he was almost the last of the thoroughgoing generalists. (The very last may be Trilling's friend and Columbia colleague Jacques Barzun, whose *From Dawn to Decadence* is an excursion through five hundred years of Western history.) The patrician Wilson, whom Trilling admired and hoped to emulate, was also among the last of the independent men of letters —a genuine free lance of uncompromised autonomy. Trilling, though, needed the security of a steady job. As a young college instructor he was for a time supporting both his ailing wife and his impoverished parents; even so, he aspired to Wilson's princely freedom. The prestige he craved, and the lusts of his ambition, were not to be satisfied by a professorship, however elevated his position eventually became. Though he did not have Wilson's elasticity—Trilling might have been incurious about the Iroquois —the mettle of his literary scrutiny, and his excavations into the meaning of culture, surpassed the scope of the academy. He was in it and yet seemed to loom somewhere beyond it. Erudition enriched his thinking, but it was intuition more than learning that pressed his sentences forward from loop to loop. He was an intellectual who wanted to be an artist.

The eclipse of an artist can sometimes be reversed (Melville and Dickinson are the famous American examples); the eclipse of an intellectual, almost never. When a society changes—and from generation to generation society always changes—art trumps time. That Anna Karenina's divorce troubles would not be likely to lead to her suicide in the twenty-first century hardly invalidates the purity of Tolstoy's masterwork. Literary intellectuals, by contrast, are singularly chained to the mood and condition of their given decades. Time may turn novels into classics; critical essays it turns into symptomatic documents of an era. In our own era, no one has supplanted Trilling, and it is easy to understand why. The study of literature no longer strives for what Trilling (in language that might invite scoffing) dared to call "moral realism." Today there is a well-known critic celebrated for aesthetic rhapsody, and countless minor zealots enmeshed in the vines of rivarous ideologies, from which too many English-department Tarzans swing. But there is no grand cultural explicator and doubter, no serious traveler to the most exalted, and often the most problematical, stations of art and ideas and manners, no public mind contemplating the transcendent through the gritty resistances of human vulnerability. Trilling was conscious of a complexity of earthbound ironies: he saw that despite the loftiness of one's will or desire, the gross and the immediate impose themselves.

"The kind of critical interest I am asking the literary intellectual to take in the life around him is a proper interest of the literary mind," he stated in 1952, in one of his more roundabout sentences, five years after he had stopped writing fiction. This was not the bright and malleable sentence of a fiction writer; it was the utterance of a figure. "Art," he ended, with his most Arnoldian gesture, "strange and sad as it may be to have to say it again, really is the criticism of life."

Criticism is the watchword. It is sad though not strange that, in the thin stream of his fiction, Trilling's narrative vigor was constrained partly by the emotionally pruned-down Hemingway example, but mainly through the absence of that tumultuous and wingèd strain that animates character and lubricates it and gives it the quiver of being. All the same, Trilling was a novelist. Or, with more novels than one to his name, could have been; and perhaps should have been. He had the psychological equipment for it. His social and historical shrewdness was steeped in experience (Whittaker Chambers was the model for Gifford Maxim of *The Middle of the Journey*), and he had, in his storytelling, a lucidly objective American voice. With a body of work behind him, the novelist he most might have resembled was William Dean Howells—of whom Trilling wrote, "we expect of him that he will involve us in the enjoyment of moral activity through the medium of a lively awareness of manners, that he will delight us by touching on high matters in the natural course of gossip." And what is this if not a sketch of Trilling's own lone novel? Defending Howells, he notes that critics have judged Howells's fiction to be "bloodless"—the very word, bitterly recorded in the notebooks, that had been applied to *The Middle of the Journey*.

Four years before his death, Trilling was invited to give a talk at Purdue University. Uncharacteristically, he chose to speak of himself:

> I am always surprised when I hear myself referred to as a critic. After some thirty years of having been called by that name, the role and the function it designates seems odd to me.
>
> I do not say alien, I only say odd. With the passing years I have learned to accept the name—to live with it, as we say— and even to be gratified by it. But it always startles me, takes me a little back . . .
>
> If I ask myself why this is so, the answer would seem to be that in some sense I did not ever undertake to be a critic. . . . The plan that did please my thought was certainly literary, but what it envisaged was the career of a novelist. To this intention, criticism, when eventually I began to practice it, was always secondary, an afterthought: in short, not a vocation but an avocation.

An astonishing public confession: the years of teaching, the years of writing, the honor and the fame that accrued in its wake —all this no more than an avocation! And the vocation? Buried.

Sad and strange as it may be to have to say it again (and who can help echoing and re-echoing Trilling's blue notes?), the whole of it, vocation and avocation, is by now defeated, buried, lost. The imposing stuff of Trilling's literary temperament, resplendent in its intellect and subtlety and style—and, dare one say, its nobility—may turn out to be no more than a reminder and a marker: a necessary headstone. Criticism of life is not seen to be the business of criticism. The demarcations of high culture have given way to the obliteration of boundaries. The figure has given way to the performer.

But suppose vocation and avocation had really been transposed, and Trilling had fulfilled his intention, leaving behind a long row of novels—novels of manners, of social observation, and (as he once characterized Howells's novels) of moderate sentiments and the sense of things? In 1976, Jacques Barzun, thinking back to the figure that was already fading a year after Trilling's death, regretted his friend's "unwarrantedly subdued reputation." If there had been more novels, he agreed (perhaps he was privy to Trilling's more intimate reflections), "or if he had spoken as a free lance instead of from an academic platform, the response might have been different—not wiser, perhaps, but louder and nearer the mark."

§

There is no long row of novels: they once existed in Trilling's fantasy; they may dimly glimmer in ours. Still, in the shoreless precincts of the essays one can hear the call, desolate but urgent, of the thinker and the teacher—and never mind that behind the scenes he disowned teaching. He may have despaired of his students, but not of ideas. What he was after, in the classroom and in the world, was the "power of supposing that ideas are real"; he was persuaded that only an "intense and ambivalent sense of history" could fuel that power. He condemned fashionable self-consciousness and self-pity, which he identified as false virtue and light resolve. He eschewed softness. He saw through "the political awareness that is not aware, the social consciousness which hates full consciousness, the moral earnestness which is moral luxury." He saw through his own time, and perhaps through ours.

Then is it possible, after all, that it is not Lionel Trilling who is buried and lost, but rather ourselves, we who relinquish his austere searchings for the sake of angry academic piddlings and ephemeral public trivia?

§

An inexorable postscript. Any mention of Trilling's name today instantly elicits the recognition that he was the first Jew appointed to Columbia University's permanent English faculty—as if this were the only significant relic of an eminent career. Trilling's triumph erupted on the heels of a humiliating dismissal; he had been fired on the ground that he was a Jew and a Marxist. Attempting to fight back, he secured painful interviews with the men who had ejected him; it was for his own good, they told him, he would not fit in. In desperation he sent a copy of his dissertation to Nicholas Murray Butler, Columbia's president. Butler chose merit over bigotry—but the harsh peril of this history left Trilling wary ever after. The young writer who was drawn to the *Menorah Journal* for its intellectual and literary standards rose to be the edgy critic who later denigrated that journal as "sterile." He was concerned with reputation and how to achieve it—how to avoid eclipse. It was lasting fame he had in mind. "I know of no writer in English," he insisted, "who has added a micromillimeter to his stature by 'realizing his Jewishness,' although I know of some who have curtailed their promise by trying to heighten their Jewish consciousness." Trilling wrote these words in 1944, when the German ovens were at full blast and European Jewish consciousness was, in the most literal sense, unrealized. He was then thirty-nine; his stature was already assured. He could not have imagined that he would come to be remembered largely, if not chiefly, as Columbia's first Jew.

TRADITION AND (OR VERSUS)
THE JEWISH WRITER

§ WHAT IS A JEWISH BOOK? A narrow definition—but also conceptually the widest—would chiefly include the Torah and the Talmud (the Hebrew Bible and the ocean of ethically transformative commentaries), and all other texts that strive to unriddle the Job-like vagaries of the human heart while urging it toward the moral life. A Jewish book is liturgy, ethics, philosophy, ontology. A Jewish book speaks of the attempt to create a world in the image of God while never presuming to image God. A Jewish book, whether it is Maimonides's *Guide for the Perplexed*, written in the twelfth century, or Joseph Soloveitchik's *The Lonely Man of Faith*, written in the twentieth, derives ultimately from the radical commandment in Leviticus, "Love thy neighbor as thyself," and from the still more radical imperative of the *Sh'ma*, the Unitary Credo.

A Jewish book is didactic. It is dedicated to the promotion of virtue attained through study. It summons obligation. It presupposes a Creator and His handiwork. Is what is popularly termed the Jewish-American novel (if in fact there exists such an entity today) likely to be a Jewish book?

I think not; indeed, I hope not. If a novel's salient aim is virtue, *I want to throw it against the wall*. It is commonly understood (never mind the bigots' immemorial canards) that to be a

Jew is to be a good citizen, to be socially responsible, to be chari-
table, to feel pity, to be principled, to stand against outrage. To be
a novelist is to be the opposite—to seize unrestraint and freedom, even demonic freedom, imagination with its reins cut loose.
The term "Jewish writer" ought to be an oxymoron. That may be
why novelists born Jewish, yet drawn wholly to the wild side—
Norman Mailer, for instance—are not altogether wrong when
they decline to be counted among Jewish writers.

What we want from novels is not what we want from the
transcendent liturgies of the synagogue. The light a genuine
novel gives out is struck off by the nightmare calculations of art:
story, language (language especially), irony, comedy, the crooked
lanes of desire and deceit.

The late Irving Howe defined the American Jewish novel (it
had not yet become the Jewish-American novel) exclusively by its
subject matter. And the Jewish novel's only viable subject matter,
he insisted, was the great crisis of immigration and its aftermath;
when that was played out, as it inevitably would be, the hands of
Jewish writers would hang empty. But the complexities of immigration and the conflicts between older and newer generations
are hardly confined to Jews, and Willa Cather's immigrant Bohemians had already made claim to that territory: so Howe's self-
imploding definition was mistaken from the start.

Still, he was right to predict an absence of Jewish subject
matter in America. The profoundly Jewish themes of our time
derive from Europe (the effect of the mass murder of one-third of
the world's Jewish population) and from the restitution of historic
Jewish sovereignty in Israel (the twentieth century's most revolutionary event, which only Philip Roth, among noted writers of
fiction, has had the wit to touch on). All other subject matter in
the so-called Jewish-American novel is, well, American, written
in the American language, telling American stories.

Multiculturalism, which is far more zealously activist than old-fashioned live-and-let-live pluralism, likes to manufacture "ethnic" fiction. (Ethnic: a sociologists' misnomer, producing fake and demeaning splintering. The word is Greek in origin, and refers to pagans—i.e., to persons neither Jewish nor Christian.) In recent decades, almost all anthologies of fiction, in order to be "inclusive," have occasionally harvested weak prose. This practice, steeped in societal good will, results in ill will toward literature. Background, however individuated, is not the same as literature. The signal Jewish luminaries of American literature today continue to be Saul Bellow and Philip Roth; no Jewish writer of their generation or the next matches them. Yet their engine and their genius have been toward the making of literature, not the expression of background. If background is powerfully there, it is because, as Isaac Bashevis Singer shrewdly put it, every writer needs to have an address. Isaac Babel had his ebullient Odessa gangsters, but also his stories of pogrom. Sholem Aleichem's shtetl terrors are masked as comedy, Singer's as demonology. Kafka's dread—the Jewish dread of the denial of the right to exist—wears the counterfeit name of justice.

But address means more than geography; it means being addressed by a literary tradition in one's own language, meaning the particular history secreted in the very syllables of language. Why else do we speak of Chekhov, Dostoyevsky, Tolstoy as Russian writers, and of Jane Austen and Dickens and George Eliot as English writers, and of Jorge Luis Borges and Gabriel García Márquez as South American writers, and so on? There is an element of instinctive coloration in being Russian, English, Argentinian, Colombian that emerges in the hidden turns of a work of literature.

And what is true of national perception and nuance is true of religious perception and nuance (even if one has given up religious identity). In this sense, John Updike is a Christian writer, V. S. Naipaul a Hindu writer, Salman Rushdie a Muslim writer. It is self-evident that any writer's subject matter will emerge from that writer's preoccupations; all writers are saturated, to one degree or another, in origins, in history. And for everyone alive in the century we have left behind, the cataclysm of murder and atrocity that we call the Holocaust is inescapable and indelible, and inevitably marks—stains—our moral nature; it is an event that excludes no one.

And yet no writer should be expected to be a moral champion or a representative of "identity." That way lies tract and sermon and polemic, or, worse yet, syrup. When a thesis or a framework—any kind of prescriptiveness or tendentiousness—is imposed on the writing of fiction, imagination flies out the door, and with it the freedom and volatility and irresponsibility that imagination both confers and commands. Writers as essayists, or polemicists, or pundits, may take on the concerns of a collectivity when they are moved to; but writers of fiction ought to be unwilling to stand for anything other than Story, however deeply they may be attached to a tradition. Tradition, to be sure, suggests a collectivity and a history, and invokes a kind of principled awareness; it carries with it a shade of teacherliness, of obligation.

But tradition is useful to the writer only insofar as the writer is unconscious of its use; only insofar as it is invisible and inaudible; only insofar as the writer breathes it in with the air; only insofar as principled awareness and teacherliness are absent; only insofar as the writer is deaf to the pressure of the collectivity. What could be more treacherous to the genuine nature of the literary impulse than to mistake the writer for a communal leader, or for the sober avatar of a glorious heritage? No writer is trustworthy or steady enough for that. The aims of imaginative writers are the aims of fiction. Not of community service or communal expectation.

Writers are responsible only to the comely shape of a sentence, and to the unfettered imagination, which sometimes leads to wild places via wild routes. At the same time one must reserve one's respect for writers who do not remain ignorant of history (a condition equal to autolobotomy), who do not choose to run after trivia, who recognize that ideas are emotions, and that emotions are ideas; and that this is what we mean when we speak of the insights of art.

HENRY JAMES, TOLSTOY, AND MY FIRST NOVEL

On NOVEMBER 22, 1963, the day President John Kennedy was assassinated, I wrote the last words of *Trust*, my first novel. I had begun it while still in my twenties, and finished it seven years later. In actuality there had been two "first" novels before then — the earlier one never completed, though it had already accumulated three hundred thousand words. I had planned it as a "philosophical" fiction; in graduate school I had come under the influence of Eliseo Vivas, at the time a well-known professor of philosophy, and with his character and views in mind, I named my protagonist Rafael Caritas. His antagonist, as I conceived it (the metaphysical versus the pragmatic), was a man of the type of Sidney Hook, a legendary figure in my undergraduate days at New York University: in my aborted novel he was called Seymour Karp. It never occurred to me — I learned it painfully years afterward — that it might be perilous to import real persons into fiction. My idea was to confront Passion with Reason. Of course I sided with Passion (I was twenty-two), which explained why a stanza from one of William Blake's "Songs of Innocence" supplied the title: *Mercy, Pity, Peace, and Love.* ("For Mercy has a human heart, / Pity a human face, / And Love, the human form divine, / And Peace, the human dress.")

Rafael Caritas consumed years before he, or I, ran out of

philosophical steam. Vivas's devotion to what he termed Neo-Thomism had befuddled me; so did his lectures on Aristotle's *Nicomachean Ethics*. What was even more confounding, though, was his fury at the Nuremberg trials. The men in the dock were wicked beyond wicked, he raged—but the Allied tribunal was wicked too: it stood for victors' justice. Then what should be done with these murderous miscreants? Punish them, Vivas said, according to a practice not unknown in certain parts of his native South America: bury each man up to his neck in earth, and send riders at a gallop to trample the exposed heads. It was an argument worthy of Dostoyevsky's Grand Inquisitor. Vivas, even when he was jovially avuncular, as he sometimes was, intimidated me: his black hair, slicked back, gleamed like shoe polish; his foreign rasp had a demonic twist; his classroom manner was a roar. Rafael Caritas was far tamer.

Mercy, Pity, Peace, and Love was slowly proceeding (though without the horsemen), pullulating with new characters I could hardly fathom or control. No resolution was anywhere in sight when I came, one afternoon, on a seductive announcement in one of the serious literary quarterlies. A publisher was soliciting short novels. Short! The word—the idea—captivated. *Mercy, Pity, Peace, and Love* was winding on and on, like a Möbius strip: where was its end? As a kind of interim project, I set out to write a short novel. It turned out to be a long one. It turned out to be *Trust*.

But *Trust* too wound on and on. All around me writers of my generation were publishing; I was not. I held it as an article of faith that if you had not attained print by twenty-five, you were inexorably marked by a scarlet F—for Folly, for Futility, for Failure. It was a wretched and envious time. I knew a writer my own age, as confident as he was industrious, who had recently completed a novel in six weeks. I was determined to emulate his feat. I threw the already massive *Trust* into a drawer and started a fresh manuscript—my second "first" novel; in a month and a half it was done. It had exhausted me, but I was also relieved and elated: I had finally finished a novel. It disappeared decades ago—lost, I believe, in the dust of a London publisher's cellar. A carbon copy (how obsolete these words are!) may be languishing in my own cellar, but I have never troubled to look for it; dead is dead. And the speedy writer I was mimicking—or hoping to rival—never published that or any other novel.

Three years elapsed between the completion of *Trust* and its appearance in print. I filled the void by writing short stories and teaching freshman composition to engineering students; but mainly I was waiting. The editor who had accepted my manuscript explained that he would soon supply "suggestions." Secretly I dreaded these—I had labored over every syllable for all those seven years—but I was wedded to diffidence and gratitude, and clearly my unpublished condition was subordinate to the editor's will, and certainly to his more pressing preoccupations. As it happened, I had acquired an agent along the way—an agent just starting out, living obscurely in a Manhattan basement. He had read a poem of mine in a literary journal, had discovered that a novel was "in progress," and offered to represent me. It was in a letter to him, after six months had passed and no suggestions were forthcoming, that I complained of the editor's silence. "I see you have clay feet," the agent wrote back, reprimanding me for untoward impatience. Another twelve months followed, and still no word from the editor. At last I made an anguished appeal, and was rewarded with a reply. He was working, the editor said, on an important book by a professor at Harvard (his name was Henry Kissinger); nevertheless he would set aside half an hour for me. He hadn't been neglectful of my manuscript, he assured me—on the contrary, for an entire year he had been compiling a long list of notes for the improvement of my novel.

The publisher's offices struck me as industrial—so many elevators, so many corridors, so many mazes and cubicles. I found the cubicle I had been directed to and looked in. There sat the editor, with a typewriter on an open leaf beside him; there on a big littered desk lay the familiar box containing my manuscript. I watched him insert a sheet of yellow paper into the machine and begin to type. "Come in," he said, seeing me hesitant in the doorway. I continued to watch him type, and all at once understood that there was no long list of notes; there had never been any notes at all; he was at that moment conjuring a handful of impromptu comments out of the air. For this I had been kept in a vise of anxiety for a year and a half.

Not long afterward, the editor, a young man still in his thirties, fell dead of a heart attack on the tennis court. Another editor took his place, and quickly put before me the first hundred pages of *Trust*, scribbled all over in red pencil. The famous suggestions! A meek petitioner facing power, I knew by now that I must succumb—I must please the new editor, or lose the chance of publication. My decision was instant. I declined every stroke of his red pencil. I believed in Art; I believed, above all, in the autonomy of Art; and for the sake of this sacral conviction I chose my novel's oblivion. Better oblivion than an alien fingerprint! To my astonishment, the new editor agreed to publish *Trust* exactly as I had written it. His name was David Segal, and like the editor who had hoodwinked me, he too died young. As for the hoodwinker, I long refused the ameliorative *de mortuis nil nisi bonum:* of the dead let nothing bad be said. Yet David Segal, as long as he lived, was wont to dismiss the good I repeatedly said of him: "You think I'm a great editor," he accused me, "because I never edited you."

Why did I believe in Art, and in the autonomy of Art, and in the sacred character of the dedicated writer? All this derived, in part, from ambition—a species of ambition that itself derived from the last trickles of the nineteenth century leaching into the twentieth. The nineteenth century did not stop abruptly in the year 1901, with the death of Queen Victoria, or the assassination of President McKinley, or the formulation of the quantum theory, or the inauguration of Picasso's Blue Period. In mores especially, the nineteenth century lingered on—even through the modernist eruptions of the twenties—into the thirties and forties, and into a portion of the fifties. In the forties song sheets could still be bought in stationery shops, and patterns for sewing dresses at home were still on sale in department stores. Secretaries wore felt hats to the office, and the rare women executives wore them *in* the office. Little girls were reading the social archaisms of the Bobbsey Twins series, and boys were immersed in the plucky if antiquated adventures of the Hardy Boys. Tabloids published one-page daily fictions called "short shorts"; big-circulation magazines unfailingly published stories. And literary ambition earnestly divided high from low, serious from popular, fiction from journalism, and novelists from the general run of mankind. (Nor was "mankind" regarded as gender-biased.) Literary writers frowned on commercial success as the antithesis of artistic probity. T. S. Eliot (despite the vastness of his own success) was the archbishop of High Art, that immaculate altar, and in his vatic wake Lionel Trilling was similarly pained by the juxtaposition of literature and money (his worship of Hemingway notwithstanding). Bohemianism meant living apart, living for art, despising Babbittry.

All these attitudes and atmospheres fell away no earlier than sixty or seventy years into the twentieth century: it took that long for nineteenth-century literary sensibilities to ebb. Modernism hardly contradicted these impressions; it confirmed and augmented them. But by the 1970s, the novel as the holy vessel of imagination (itself having deposed poetry) was undone. Magazines dropped fiction. Notions of journalism as the equal of imaginative writing took hold ("the nonfiction novel," pioneered by Truman Capote, replicated by Norman Mailer). Bohemians who had been willing enough to endure the romantic penury of cold-water walkups while sneering at popular entertainment were displaced by beatniks who were themselves popular entertainment. Walt Whitman was transmogrified into Allen Ginsberg and Jack Kerouac. From *beat* you were to infer *beatific*, and the New Age of faux mysticism (via hallucinogens) had begun. New theories leveled the literary terrain—so that, visiting Yale a decade or so ago, I was startled to encounter a young professor of English deconstructing a hamburger advertisement with the same gravity as an earlier professoriat would have devoted to a discussion of *Paradise Lost*.

With such radical (and representative) changes in the culture, and with High Art in the form of the novel having lost its centrality, the nature of ambition too was bound to alter. This is not to say that young writers today are no longer driven—and some may even be possessed—by the strenuous forces of literary ambition. Zeal, after all, is a constant, and so must be the pool, or the sea, of born writers. But the great engines of technology lure striving talents to television and Hollywood, or to the lighter varieties of theater, or (especially) to the prompt gratifications and high-velocity fame of the magazines, where topical articles generate buzz and gather no moss. The sworn novelists, who, despite the devourings of the hour, continue to revere the novel (the novel as moss, with its leisurely accretions of character and incident, its disclosures of secrets, its landscapes and cityscapes and mindscapes, its idiosyncratic particularisms of language and insight)—these sworn novelists remain on the scene, if not on the rise.

Still, there is a difference. The altars are gone. The priests are dead. Writers and artists of all kinds are no longer publicly or privately abashed by the rewards of commerce. The arbiters of literary culture have either departed (few remember Irving Howe, say, or Randall Jarrell) or have devolved into popular celebrities, half sage, half buffoon.

When I began *Trust*, close to fifty years ago, ambition meant what James Joyce had pronounced it to be, in a mantra that has inflamed generations: *silence, exile, and cunning*. Silence and exile were self-explanatory: the novelist was to be shut away in belief—self-belief, perhaps—and also in the monkish conviction that Literature was All. But cunning implied something more than mere guile. It hinted at power, power sublime and supernal, the holy power of language and its cadences—the sentence, the phrase, and ultimately, primordially, the word: the germ of being. As chosen sibyl of the word, I was scornful of so-called writers who produced "drafts," in the shape of an imperfect spew to be returned to later, in order, as one novelist described it, "to polish the verbal surface." The verbal surface! The word could no more be defined by its surface than the sea could be fathomed by its coastline; and I could no more abandon a sentence, even temporarily, than I could skip a substantial interval of breathing with a promise to make up for it afterward. Until the sentence, the phrase, the word were as satisfactorily woven as the weaver's shuttle could thread them, I would not tread further: in Henry James's formulation, "the finer thread, the tighter weave." Or recall Jacob's struggle with the angel: "I will not let thee go, except thou bless me." Until I felt its nimbus, I would not let any cluster of words go.

It was slow work, and it owed more to Henry James than it did to the angel of Genesis. I kept on my writing table (a worn old hand-me-down, three feet by one and a half, that I had acquired at age eight) a copy of *The Ambassadors*, as a kind of talisman. I kept it there not so much for the sake of James's late prose (though it often seemed that his penchant for intrusively inter-locutory adverbs seeped into my fountain pen's rubber ink blad-der) as for the scent of ambition: the worldliness of his characters, the visual brilliance of his long scenes, the seductiveness of his be-trayals, the veiled innocence of his young women, the subtlety of his moral conundrums, and not least his debt to human possibil-ity, and also to human taint. His muse was tragic; and so was mine. What James felt in his worship of Balzac was what I suf-fered in my fealty to James: Balzac appeared to him "so multitudi-nous, so complex, so far-spreading, so suggestive, so portentous —... such misty edges and far reverberations—that the imagina-tion, oppressed and overwhelmed, shrinks from any attempt to grasp it whole." Yet it was just this multitudinousness, this com-plexity, this far-spreadingness I was after. I named my novel *Trust* with biting intent: it was to denote a vast and cynical irony. I meant to map every species of *dis*trust—between parent and child; between husband and wife; between lovers; between Eu-rope and America; between Christians and Jews; between God and man; in politics and in history. Before the term Holocaust was put to use or even known, the death camps entered *Trust;* in 1957, scarcely a decade after the ovens had cooled, who could fail to address them? (Many did.) Enoch Vand, my protagonist's step-father, confronting the goddess Geopolitica, records the names of the victims in masses of ledgers:

> And he could not confess for the sake of whom or what he dug down deep in those awesome volumes, sifting their name-burdened and number-laden leaves as soil is spaded and weighed in search of sunken graves and bones time-turned to stone—he could not say or tell. . . . Enoch leaned brooding among the paper remnants of the damned: the lists and questionnaires, the numbers and their nemeses; every

table spread with the worms' feast; the room a registry and bursary for smoke and cinders. Over it all his goddess hung. If she wore a pair of bucklers for her breasts, they gleamed for him and shimmered sound like struck cymbals; if slow vein-blood drooped like pendants from her gored ears, they seemed to him jewels more gradual than pearls—she formed herself out of the slaughter, the scarves and winds of smoke met to make her hair, the cinders clustered to make her thighs; she was war, death, blood, perpetual misbirths; she came up enlightened from that slaughter like a swimmer from the towering water-wall with his glorified face; she came up an angel from that slaughter and the fire-whitened cinders of those names. She came up Europa.

And elsewhere, the meditation of a refugee from Vienna, reduced in exile to a servant:

Grit is one of the eternals. The chimneys heave their laden bladders, the grit is spawned out of a domestic cloud in the lowest air, the black footless ants appear on the sill. Brush away, mop away, empty buckets with zeal; grit returns. Everything is flux; grit is forever. Futility is day after day. Time is not what we suppose, moments in an infinite queue, but rather a heavy sense that we have been here before, only with hope, and are here again, only without it. "Your luck will not change," says Time, "give up, the world has concerns of its own," says Time, "woe cannot be shared," says Time, "regret above all is terrifyingly individual." And Time says, "Take no comfort in your metaphysics of the immortality of the race. When your species has evolved out of recognition grit will be unspoiled. There will always be grit. It alone endures. It is greater than humanity."

But it is not greater than humanity; it is the same. We join the particles in their dance on the sill. It is the magnificent

Criminal plan, to shove us into the side of a hill, mulch us until we are dissolved into something more useful but less spectacular than before, and send us out again in the form of a
cinder for some churl of a descendant to catch in his eye,
cursing. . . . Who can revere a universe which will take that
lovely marvel, man (after all the fierce mathematics that went
into him, aeons of fish straining toward the dry, gill into
lung, paw into the violinist's and the dentist's hand), and turn
him into a carbon speck?

Of course none of this can be construed as Jamesian. Perhaps, after all, such passages carry, rather, the spirit of Ecclesiastes
(or, as some may say, the Book of Fustian). In any case, *Trust* in its
voraciousness went everywhere. It went into verses and puns; its
population proliferated—lawyers, editors, diplomats, nannies,
colonels, schoolgirls; it grew limbs of metaphor and Medusa-
heads of dialogue; it wandered toward the lyrical-mystical in an
apostrophe to a tree. It set out, in raw competitiveness, to rival
the burgeoning sexual openness of the late fifties—and also to
deride, twenty years in advance of it, William Gass's 1976 dictum
that women "lack that blood-congested genital drive" that is at
the root of style. An early reviewer, writing not in unstinting
praise, nevertheless acknowledged "evidence of extraordinary
ambition in the scope of the novel," and remarked that "the long
visionary account of the love-making between the heroine's father and a young woman surpasses anything Mailer has ever
done, indeed is managed with the ingenuity and resourcefulness
of a French cineaste." To be fair, this same reviewer "frankly con-
fess[ed] that the novel gave me little pleasure."

Recently I reread—for the first time since high school—
William Dean Howells's *The Rise of Silas Lapham*. Here was a
novel that gave me great pleasure: the prose plain and direct, the
characters lifelike, engaging, trustworthy, the plotting realisti-

cally plausible and gratifyingly suspenseful. All the same, when you compare Howells with James, the disparity of mind and sensibility—what each man aspired to, or could attain—arouses a perplexity. How could these two have been, as they were, literary companions? Howells occupies a few well-spent hours;* James (like the far more visceral Conrad) seizes your life. That seizure, I suppose, points to the kind of ambition I fastened on in my twenties. In those years my hungriest uncle (hungry in every sense: one of five, he was the only one who attempted to feed his family by means of his pen) was still living: he was a poet. Matchless in three languages, he chose to make his mark in Hebrew. His poetry was complex, visionary, hugely erudite, with, here and there, noble biblical resonances and classical turns that recalled, to an eminent literary critic, Milton and Shelley. Some of my uncle's work he himself rendered into English; but when any eagerly willing translator approached him, he drove the hapless volunteer off with arrogant scorn; he recognized no peer; he had a consciousness of anointment. I will wait, he announced, *a thousand years* for the right translator! Today my uncle is unknown; his life's achievement is in blackest obscurity.

That superannuated consciousness of anointment has also long been obscured—to speak of it now is likely to induce derision. But surely Joyce had it, unalloyed, in writing *Ulysses*, and particularly in the esoteric labors of *Finnegans Wake*; and James

---

* Since writing these words, I have eagerly returned to Howells. Any reader familiar with, say, *A Modern Instance*, or *A Hazard of New Fortunes*, will repudiate, as I emphatically do now, this disparagement of a neglected American luminary. In intellect and wit, in judgment and insight, in apperception of moral violence, Howells is easily James's penetrating comrade; and surely they are equal practitioners of the fiction of manners. Where Howells differs from James is in a kind of stoic recognition (or resignation) that things are what they must be—whereas in James tragedy is starkly, darkly irredeemable, least of all by philosophical serenity.

had it, shadowed in his final years by the failure of his New York Edition, designed to consolidate his stature; and among contemporary American writers it can be descried in Updike, Roth, and Bellow—all of whom began in the penumbra of nineteenth-century literary ambition, which has long masqueraded as modernism.

Trust was written in that same penumbra, with that same consciousness of anointment, though its shadowy fate, despite a handful of paperback reissues over the years, mostly resembles that of my uncle's grandly bedizened stanzas. Nearly four decades have passed since my first novel first saw print. Perhaps my style has grown plainer as I have grown older; perhaps not. But surely I have acquiesced in the alterations of the common literary culture.

And here it is needful to recall a hiatus—a cut that fell like an ax. Sometime in the seventies, the old ambition was routed by an invader called the *nouveau roman*. Its name was French because its inventors and original practitioners were French: most prominently, Alain Robbe-Grillet and Nathalie Sarraute. Their idea of the novel turned out to be nothing more than a fad, a brutalizing one, touted by a few influential American critics writing in advanced periodicals with the intention of shaming the traditional novel out of existence. I cannot now reconstruct or characterize this "new novel," except out of a wash of ebbing memory. It was icily detached; it was "objective" and unsentimental; it cared more for space and time than for stories or souls; its bloodless aesthetic was minutely deadpan; its dialogue tended to be expressed in arid aperçus; often it read like a stilted translation of Roland Barthes. And finally it was repudiated by its chief American promulgator, who, as if by imperial fiat, rehabilitated what had been, as if by imperial fiat, imposed. For fiction writers who resisted being drawn into the tide of literary pronouncements from above (or who were temperamentally alien to it), it was an enervating and marginalizing season.

Ephemeral though they were, these new pieties and prescriptions did throw a light on the nature of the old ambition. The *nouveau roman* arrived as an extension of cultural power by a coterie of celebrated literary figures determined to wield it. The introduction of literary philosophies from abroad aimed to force an avant-garde: those who declined to follow were dismissed as either obsolete or mediocre. As God had been declared dead by certain theologians, so now was the novel—the novel as it had been understood and illumined from, say, Tolstoy to E. M. Forster, or from Virginia Woolf to Faulkner; or, in any event, before Robbe-Grillet. But the old ambition of the penumbra had been hammered out of the self, bare of any desire for social or cultural hegemony. It asserted its conviction of hard-won ownership, from which derived its authority; but it was the authority of innerness, of interior powers wrested out of language itself. By contrast, it was critical will alone that fueled the *nouveau roman*. The novels of its fashionable American disciples were critics' novels. No one can say that they died with a whimper—even a whimper requires a pulse.

If I press on in homage to the old ambition, I intend more than praise for writers' limitless appetite. I am thinking of readers. Here, then, is a very long paragraph, written in 1909:

> I was returning home by the fields. It was midsummer; the hay harvest was over, and they were just beginning to reap the rye. At that season of the year there is a delightful variety of flowers—red, white and pink scented tufty clover; milk-white ox-eye daisies with their bright yellow centers and pleasant spicy smell; yellow honey-scented rape blossoms, tall campanulas with white and lilac bells, tulip-shaped;

creeping vetch; yellow, red and pink scabious; plantains with faintly scented, neatly arranged purple, slightly pink-tinged blossoms; cornflowers, bright blue in the sunshine and while still young, but growing paler and redder towards evening or when growing old; and delicate quickly withering almond-scented dodder flowers. I gathered a large nosegay of these different flowers, and was going home, when I noticed in a ditch, in full bloom, a beautiful thistle plant of the crimson kind, which in our neighborhood they call "Tartar," and carefully avoid when mowing—and if they do happen to cut it down, throw out from among the grass from fear of pricking their hands. Thinking to pick this thistle and put it in the center of my nosegay, I climbed down into the ditch, and, after driving away a velvety humble-bee that had penetrated deep into one of the flowers and . . .

But the paragraph, though it goes on well beyond this, must be interrupted. It is the start of Tolstoy's *Hadji Murad*, in Aylmer Maude's translation. (My uncle's poetry was composed rather in this vein.) I interrupt the paragraph for two reasons—first, because of what must appear to be gargantuan hubris: what is a passage from Tolstoy, the pinnacle of all novelists, doing here, in these ruminations on an emphatically inconspicuous work by an emphatically unnoticed young writer holed up almost half a century ago in a little house at the farthest margin of the Bronx? It is precisely for the sake of hubris that it is here. Without it, how can I lay out the untamed lustful graspingness, the secret tough-hearted avarice, of the old ambition?

More than twenty years ago, in an essay called "The Lesson of the Master," I bitterly excoriated that ambition:

The true Lesson of the Master, then, is, simply, never to venerate what is complete, burnished, whole, in its grand organic flowering or finish—never to look toward the admirable and dazzling end; never to be ravished by the goal; never to worship ripe Art or the ripened artist; but instead to seek to be young while young, primitive while primitive, ungainly while ungainly—to look for crudeness and rudeness, to husband one's own stupidity or ungenius.

There *is* this mixup most of us have between ourselves and what we admire or triumphantly cherish. We see this mixup, this mishap, this mishmash, most often in writers: the writer of a new generation ravished by the genius writer of a classical generation, who begins to dream herself, or himself, as powerful, vigorous and original—as if being filled up by the genius writer's images, scenes, and stratagems were the same as having the capacity to pull off the identical magic. . . . If I were twenty-two now, I would not undertake a cannibalistically ambitious Jamesian novel to begin with; I would look into the eyes of Henry James at twenty-two. . . . It is not to the Master in his fullness I would give my awed, stricken, desperate fealty, but to the faltering, imperfect, dreaming youth.

All this I now repudiate and recant. There is too much humility in it—and humility is for the aging, not for the young. Obsequiousness at any age is an ugly thing, and ugliest in that early time of youthful hope. At twenty-two one *ought* to be a literary voluptuary; one *ought* to cannibalize the world.

Hence my second reason for breaking off a luxuriant Tolstoyan scene. It is because of the contemporary reader's impatience. The old ambition had reflected back to it readers who were equally covetous—but as the old ambition has faded, so has readers' craving: recognizable bookish voluptuaries and print-cannibals are rare. Readers nowadays will hardly tolerate long blocks of print unbroken by dialogue or action, and if there are to be long blocks of print at all, they must be in familiar, speedy, colloquial, undemanding prose. Are cinema and television to blame? In part. Novelists have learned much from visual technology, especially the skill of rapid juxtaposition. But film itself is heir to the more contemplative old ambition: what else is "panning," whether of a landscape or a human face? When film is on occasion gazeful, meticulous, attentive to the silent naming of things seen, its debt to the word is keenest.

Then exaltations and panegyrics for the altar and the sibyl! For consciousness of anointment (however mistaken or futile), for self-belief subversive of commerce (or call it arrogance defeated by commerce); and for *spectacle, dominion, energy and honor* —a glorifying phrase pinched from *Trust*. It was the novel of my prime; I will never again write with so hubristic a passion. It marked the crest of life, the old ambition's deepest bite—before doubt and diffidence set in, and the erosion of confidence, and the diminution of nerve. My loyalty to my first novel continues undiminished. If, in 1966, it gave no pleasure to a reviewer (except for the sex chapter), I will not complain. For the real right reader I am willing to wait a thousand years!—because it is not so much the novel that takes my praise as that archaic penumbra, that bottomless lordly overbearing ambition of long ago. Ambition as it once was.

Let Enoch Vand, chanting his imperious aphorisms in chapter twenty-two, speak for the author of *Trust* in her twenties, and a little beyond:

> To desire to be what one can be is purpose in life.
> There are no exterior forces. There are only interior forces.
> Who squanders talent praises death.

I was never again so heedlessly brave.

HIGHBROW
BLUES

§ NOT VERY LONG AGO, when the (literary) writer Jonathan Franzen was catapulted to the status of celebrity, it was not only because his novel *The Corrections* had become a bestseller. It was because he had *declined* celebrity, he had scorned it, he had thumbed his nose at it. It was because for him celebrity was a scandal, an embarrassment. It shamed him. It demeaned him. It was the opposite of his desire. His desire was to be counted among artists, not to be interviewed by a popular sentimentalist hosting a television show. His bailiwick, his turf, his lingo—his art—was serious literature. He wanted it plainly understood that he was not your run-of-the-mill Oprah pick. He was a highbrow. Oprah Winfrey, he complained, was in the habit of choosing "schmaltzy, one-dimensional" books that made him "cringe."

And then followed what may turn out to be the most arresting literary gaffe of the twenty-first century so far: "I feel," he said, "like I'm solidly in the high-art literary tradition." For a writer in that tradition, he intimated, the letter "O" (for Oprah) branded on a book jacket might signify hundreds of thousands of copies in print, but it was also the mark of Cain. Or else it was the scarlet letter of literary disgrace.

Like I'm solidly in the high-art literary tradition. Never mind that "the high-art literary tradition" generally shuns the use of "like" as a conjunction: the remark was off the cuff, presumably under a journalist's pressure, and nothing if not informal. It was the telltale phrase itself—*the high-art literary tradition*—that shot Franzen through the cannon of doleful celebrity, if not into the Western canon. What did it mean? What was it? Why did it sound so awkward, so out of tune, so self-conscious, so—one hesitates to say—jejune? Why did it have the effect of a very young man attempting to talk like the grownups? And what had become of those grownups anyhow? Why were they, by and large, no longer on the scene—so little on the scene, in fact, and so little in anyone's thoughts or vocabulary, that a locution like *high-art literary tradition* took on the chirp of mimicry, of archaism?

Poor Franzen was scolded all around. He was scolded for ingratitude. He was scolded for elitism. He was scolded for chutzpah—what sane writer would be so unreasonable as to give the cold shoulder to the powerfully influential Oprah Book Club? Even Harold Bloom scolded him. Oprah herself didn't scold him —she simply canceled him.

Only a short while before the Franzen brouhaha, Philip Roth published a little volume called *Shop Talk: A Writer and His Colleagues and Their Work*. Roth, of course, had long ago passed from the shock-celebrity, or notoriety, of *Portnoy's Complaint* to innumerable high-art literary awards, including the Gold Medal in Fiction of the American Academy of Arts and Letters. *Shop Talk* consists of interviews, exchanges, reflections: on Primo Levi, Aharon Appelfeld, Ivan Klíma, Isaac Bashevis Singer, Bruno Schulz, Milan Kundera, Edna O'Brien, Mary McCarthy, and Bernard Malamud. It closes with "Rereading Saul Bellow," a remarkable essay of homage expressed in an authoritative prose of matchless literary appetite. A writer of Roth's stature—one of the shapers of the novel in our time—engaging with ten of the significant literary figures of the twentieth century!

Fifty years ago, we can be sure, this would have been taken as an Event, as a cultural marker, as an occasion for heating up New York's literary stewpots as much as, or even more than, Franzen's explosive—and ephemeral—wistfulness. Fifty years ago, the publication of *Shop Talk* would have been the topic of scores of graduate-student warrens and middle-class dinner parties, of book and gossip columns, of the roiling cenacles of the envious ambitious bookish young. Fifty years ago, Roth's newly revealed correspondence with Mary McCarthy—in which she asserts that Roth's appraisal of anti-Semitism in *The Counterlife* "irritated and offended" her; in which she considers the "Wailing Wall" to be "repellent"; in which she wryly adds that she looks forward to Roth's conversion to Christianity—fifty years ago, these words, had they then been in print, would have engendered cool rebuttals in *Commentary*, and everywhere else a slew of op-eds, combative or conciliatory. For an analogy, only recall the storm that greeted Hannah Arendt's *Eichmann in Jerusalem:* the avalanche of editorials, the tumult of answering essays pro and con. (Mary McCarthy's pro among them.)

Some are old enough to remember the contentious excitements that surrounded the publication of Norman Mailer's *Advertisements for Myself*, a personal assessment, like *Shop Talk*, of contemporary writers. Mailer's book was far less serious, far less well intended: it was mainly a noisy, nasty, competitive display of putdowns; an audacious act of flashy self-confessed self-aggrandizement. But—like *Shop Talk*—it was, after all, about writers, and there was a zealous public for it, a public drawn to substantive literary commotion. In contrast, when *Shop Talk* appeared in the first year of the twenty-first century, its reception was nearly total muteness. *Publishers Weekly*, taking obligatory notice, denigrated this large-hearted, illuminating, selfless work of cultural inquiry and fiercely generous admiration as fresh evidence of the Rothian ego—a viewpoint false, stale, and impertinent in both senses. Perhaps there were other reviews; perhaps not. What is notable is that *Shop Talk* was not notable. It was born into silence. It attracted no major attention, or no attention at all—not even among the editors of intellectual journals. No one praised it, no one condemned it. Not a literary creature stirred in response—not even a louse.

These observations are hardly new; but familiarity does not lessen the shock and the ignominy of a pervasive indifference to serious critical writing. Fifty years ago, it was still taken for granted that there would be serious discourse about serious writing by nonprofessionals, by people for whom books were common currency. These people also listened to Jack Benny on the radio and went to the movies. I am reminded of the Reader's Subscription, a book club presided over by an astonishing highbrow triumvirate: W. H. Auden, Jacques Barzun, and Lionel Trilling. Fifty years ago, no one spoke so blatantly, so dreamily, of *the high-art literary tradition*—one doesn't give a name to the air one breathes. If the phrase sounds nostalgic today (and it does), it is because it has the awed, wondering, adoring and somewhat soppy tone Oprah herself would use; or else the tone of someone born too late, like an antiques-besotted client of limited means whom an interior decorator will oblige with duplicates of period furnishings. *The high-art literary tradition*—utter these syllables, and you utter a stage set.

In 1952, William Phillips wrote of "the attitude of aesthetic loneliness and revolt"—setting the writer apart from mass culture—that had characterized his youth. "Along with many other people, most of them more mature than myself," he said, "I felt that art was a temple and that artists belonged to a priesthood of the anointed and the dedicated." The politics and social commitment of the thirties swept all that inherited romanticism away, but only temporarily—it re-emerged soon enough in the postwar aestheticism of the New Criticism. By the 1950s, the idea of literature as hermetically dedicated and anointed was once again solidly enthroned, complete with Eliot as pope and Pound as high priest—until a second political wave, in the late sixties and into the seventies, knocked out notions of temples and priestly artists once and for all, and replaced them with a howl. It is a long time since we fretted over mass culture. It is a long time since we were thrilled by alienation. It is a long time since Dwight Macdonald sneered at middlebrows. It is a long time since Lionel Trilling thought writing for money cheapened literary aspiration. (Henry James didn't think that.) Modernism as a credo seems faded and old-fashioned, if not obsolete, and what we once called the avant-garde is now either fakery or comedy. The Village, where Auden and Marianne Moore once lived and wrote and walked abroad, is a sort of performance arena nowadays, where the memory of a memory grows fainter and fainter, and where even nostalgia has forgotten exactly what it is supposed to be nostalgic about. Distinction-making, even distinction-discerning, is largely in decline. The difference between high and low is valued by few and blurred by most. *The high-art literary tradition* brings on snickers (except when it is in the newly aspiring hands of Oprah, who, having canceled Franzen yet learned his lesson well, has ascended, together with her fans, to *Anna Karenina* and Faulkner).

Writers shouldn't be mistaken for priests, it goes without saying; but neither should movie-script manufacturers be mistaken for writers. Readers are not the same as audiences, and the structure of a novel is not the same as the structure of a lingerie advertisement. Hierarchy, to be sure, is an off-putting notion, invoking high and low; and high smacks of snobbery and antiegalitarianism. But hierarchy also points to the recognition of distinctions, and—incontrovertibly—the life of intellect is perforce hierarchical: it insists that one thing is not the same as another thing. A novel concerned with English country-house romances is not the same as a tract on slavery in Antigua. A department of English is not the same as a Marxist tutorial. A rap CD is not the same as academic scholarship. A suicide bomber who blows up a pizzeria crowded with baby carriages is not the same as a nation-builder.

Fifty years ago, a salient issue was the bugaboo of conformism. It's true that men in their universal gray fedoras had the look of a field of dandelions gone to seed. It's true that McCarthyism suppressed free opinion and stimulated fear. But both the fedoras and the unruly senator have long been dispatched to their respective graveyards, and if we are to worry about conformism, now is the hour. What does conformism mean if not one side, one argument, one solution? And no one is more conformist than the self-defined alienated, hoary though that term is. In the universities, a literary conformism rules, equating literature with fashionable "progressive" themes; and literature departments promote the newfangled conformism that paradoxically goes under the pluralist-sounding yet absolutist name of multiculturalism: a system of ethnological classification designed to reduce literary culture to group rivalries. Postcolonial courses offer a study in specified villainies and grievances. Certain imprimatur-bearing texts—ah, *texts*, denatured but indispensable coin!—are offered uncritically, as holy writ, without opposing or dissenting or contextual matter. Yet more than fifty years ago, in my freshman year at NYU, Friedrich Hayek's *The Road to Serfdom* was assigned to be read together with its antithesis, *The Communist Manifesto*—and that was in the heart of what even its denizens dubbed the Age of Conformity.

"It is worth something," Norman Mailer wrote in 1952, "to remind ourselves that the great artists—certainly the moderns—are almost always in opposition to their society, and that integration, acceptance, non-alienation, etc., has been more conducive to propaganda than art." No statement could be staler than this one, and it was already stale when it was first set down. Is the Thomas Mann of the Joseph novels an artist in opposition? Is *Dubliners* a work of revolt? What we can say with certainty is that much current study of the great artists tends to make art secondary to propaganda, and sometimes invisible under propaganda's obscuring film. In a democratic polity possessed of free critical expression through innumerable outlets, the moribund old cry of alienation is itself a species of propaganda. Nor, as that propaganda would have it, is self-congratulatory jingoism the opposite of alienation. What the propaganda of alienation seeks is not the higher patriotism saturated in the higher morality, as it pretends, but simple disinheritance.

Admittedly, there is always a golden age, the one not ours, the one that once was or will someday be. One's own time is never satisfactory, except to the very rich or the smugly oblivious. So it is doubtful that *the high-art literary tradition*, in strict opposition to mass culture, will ever return, even for its would-be latter-day avatars: high and low are inextricably intermingled, whether by sly allusion in *The Simpsons*, or in Philip Roth's dazzling demotic voice. Low has enriched high; and surely Oprah has enriched publishers. But nothing gives us license, even in the face of this enlivening cultural mishmash, to fall into meltdown: to think that a comic-strip balloon is as legitimate a "text" as *Paradise Lost;* or that the faddishly softening politics of what is misleadingly called "narrative" can negate a documented historical record; or that art exists chiefly to serve grievance. Alienation, that old carcass, remains, after all, the philistinism of the intellectual. As for the attention given decades ago to *Advertisements for Myself:* if it were published today, would anyone notice?

THE DIN
IN THE HEAD

§ ON A GRAY AFTERNOON I sit in a silent room and contemplate din. In the street a single car passes—a rapid bass vowel—and then it is quiet again. So what is this uproar, this hubbub, this heaving rumble of zigzag static I keep hearing? This echo chamber spooling out spirals of chaos? An unmistakable noise as clearly mine as fingerprint or twist of DNA: the thrum of regret, of memory, of defeat, of mutability, of bitter fear, made up of shame and ambition and anger and vanity and wishing. The soundtrack of a movie of the future, an anticipatory ribbon of scenes long dreaded, or daydreams without a prayer of materializing. Or else: the replay of unforgotten conversations, humiliating, awkward, indelible. Mainly it is the buzz of the inescapably mundane, the little daily voice that insists and insists: *right now, not now, too late, too soon, why not, better not, turn it on, turn it off, notice this, notice that, be sure to take care of, remember not to.* The nonstop chatter that gossips, worries, envies, invokes, yearns, condemns, self-condemns.

But innerness—this persistent internal hum—is more than lamentation and desire. It is the quiver of intuition that catches experience and draws it close, to be examined, interpreted, judged. Innerness is discernment; penetration; imagination; self-knowledge. The inner life is the enemy of crowds, because the life of crowds snuffs the mind's murmurings. Mind is many-threaded, mazy, meandering, while every crowd turns out to be a machine—a collectivity of parts united as to purpose.

And with the ratcheting up of technology, every machine turns out to be a crowd. All these contemporary story-grinding contrivances and appliances that purport to capture, sometimes to mimic, the inner life—what are they, really, if not the brute extrusions of the principle of Crowd? Films, with their scores of collaborators, belong to crowds. Films are addressed to crowds (even if you are alone in front of your TV screen). As for those other machine-generated probings—television confessionals, radio psychologists, telephone marketing quizzers, the retrograde e-mail contagion that reduces letter-writing to stunted nineteenth-century telegraphese, electronic "chat rooms" and "blogs" and "magazines" that debase discourse through hollow breeziness and the incessant scramble for the cutting edge—what are they, really, if not the dwarfing gyrations of crowds? Superhero cybernetics, but lacking flight. Picture Clark Kent entering a handy telephone booth not to rise up as a universal god, but to sidle out diminished and stuttering, still wearing his glasses and hat. The very disappearance of telephone booths—those private cells for the whisperings of lovers and conspirators—serves the mentality of crowds, where ubiquitously public cell phones announce confidential assignations to the teeming streets.

Tête-à-tête gone flagrante delicto.

Yet there remains a countervailing power. Its sign blazes from the title of Thomas Hardy's depiction of the English countryside, with its lost old phrase: *Far from the Madding Crowd*. How, in this madding American hour, to put a distance between the frenzy of crowds and the mind's whispered necessities? Get thee to the novel!—the novel, that word-woven submarine, piloted by intimation and intuition, that will dive you to the deeps of the heart's maelstrom.

The electronic revolution, with its accelerating development of this or that apparatus, is frequently compared to the invention of movable type — but the digital is antithetical to the inward life of letters. Print first made possible the individual's solitary engagement with an intimate text; the Gutenberg era moved human awareness from the collective to the reflective. Electronic devices promote the collective, the much-touted "global community" — again the crowd. Microchip chat employs a ghostly simulacrum of print, but chat is not an essay. Film reels out plots, but a movie is not a novel. The inner life dwells elsewhere, occasionally depositing its conscious vibrations in what we think of as the "personal" essay. Though journalism floods us with masses of articles — verbal packets of information suitable to crowds — there are, nowadays, few essays of the meditative kind.

And what of the utterly free precincts of the novel? Is the literary novel, like the personal essay, in danger of obsolescence? An academic alarm goes up every so often, and I suppose the novel may fall out of luck or fashion, at least in the long run. Where, after all, are the sovereign forms of yesteryear — the epic, the saga, the Byronic narrative poem, the autobiographical Wordsworthian ode? Literary grandeur is out of style. If Melville lived among us, would he dare to grapple with the mammoth rhapsody that is *Moby-Dick*? Forms and genres, like all breathing things, have their natural life spans. They are born into a set of societal conditions and become moribund when those conditions attenuate. But if the novel were to wither — if, say, it metamorphosed altogether into a species of journalism or movies, as many popular novels already have — then the last trustworthy vessel of the inner life (aside from our heads) would crumble away.

The novel has not withered; it holds on, held in the warmth of the hand. "It can do simply everything," Henry James wrote a century ago, "and that is its strength and its life. Its plasticity, its elasticity is infinite." These words appeared under the head "The Future of the Novel." There are advanced minds who may wish to apply them to the Internet—with predictive truth, no doubt, on their side. Communications technology may indeed widen and widen, and in ways beyond even our current fantasies. But the novel commands a realm far more perceptive than the "exchange of ideas" that, in familiar lingo, is heralded as communication, and means only what the crowd knows. Talk-show hosts who stimulate the public outpourings of the injured are themselves hedged behind the inquisitive sympathy of crowds, which is no sympathy at all. Downloading specialized knowledge—one of the encyclopedic triumphs of communications technology—is an act equal in practicality to a wooden leg; it will support your standing in the world, but there is no blood in it.

What does the novel know? It has no practical or educational aim; yet it knows what ordinary knowledge cannot seize. The novel's intricate tangle of character-and-incident alights on the senses with a hundred cobwebby knowings fanning their tiny threads, stirring up nuances and disclosures. The arcane designs and driftings of metaphor—what James called the figure in the carpet, what Keats called negative capability, what Kafka called explaining the inexplicable—are what the novel knows. It can make sentient even the furniture in a room:

> Pavel Petrovich meanwhile had gone back to his elegant study. Its walls were covered with grayish wallpaper and hung with an assortment of weapons on a many-hued Persian tapestry. The walnut furniture was upholstered in dark green

velvet. There was a Renaissance bookcase of old black oak, bronze statuettes on the magnificent writing-table, an open hearth. He threw himself on the sofa, clasped his hands behind his head and remained motionless, staring at the ceiling with an expression verging on despair. Perhaps because he wanted to hide from the very walls what was reflected in his face, or for some other reason—anyway, he got up, unfastened the heavy window curtains and threw himself back on the sofa.

That is Turgenev. A modernist would have omitted that "expression verging on despair." The despair is in the wallpaper, as Turgenev hinted; it was the literary habits of the nineteenth century that made him say the word outright. Virginia Woolf's wallpaper is sentient, too—though, because she is a modernist, she never explicitly names its mood:

> Only through the rusty hinges and swollen sea-moistened woodwork certain airs, detached from the body of the wind (the house was ramshackle after all) crept round corners and ventured indoors. Almost one might imagine them, as they entered the drawing-room questioning and wondering, toying with the flaps of the wallpaper, asking, would it hang much longer, when will it fall? Then smoothly brushing the walls, they passed on musingly as if asking the red and yellow roses on the wallpaper whether they would fade, questioning (gently, for there was time at their disposal) the torn letters in the waste-paper basket, the flowers, the books, all of which were open to them and asking, Were they allies? Were they enemies? How long would they endure?

Two small portraits, each of a room—but the subject of both (if such wavering tendrils of sensation can be termed a subject) is incorporeal, intuitional, deeply interior. A weight of sorrow inheres in Turgenev's heavy black bookcase; the feather-tap of the ephemeral touches Woolf's torn letters. And both scenes breathe out the one primordial cry: Life! Life!

Life — the inner life — is not in the production of story lines alone, or movies would suffice. The micro-universe of the modem? Never mind. The secret voices in the marrow elude these multiplying high-tech implements that facilitate the spread of information. (High tech! Facilitate the spread of information! The jargon of the wooden leg, the wooden tongue.) The din in our heads, that relentless inward hum of fragility and hope and transcendence and dread — where, in an age of machines addressing crowds, and crowds mad for machines, can it be found? In the art of the novel; in the novel's infinity of plasticity and elasticity; in a flap of imaginary wallpaper. And nowhere else.

The Rule
of the Bus

Toward the close of *Reading Lolita in Tehran*, her troubled yet inspiriting memoir of life under the ayatollahs, Azar Nafisi recounts the course of an attempted massacre. Twenty-one writers, members of the Iranian writers' association, had been invited to attend a literary conference in Armenia. Government agents at first discouraged the trip, then appeared to relent. The long bus journey had stretched well into the night, with most of the travelers asleep in their seats, when an alert passenger all at once became aware that the driver was missing and the bus was motionless: it had been abandoned at the brink of a precipice. Someone seized the wheel and swerved the vehicle out of danger. As the dazed writers emerged, the security forces who had been posted at the site beforehand—to "discover" the unfortunate "accident"—sped forward to arrest them. A plot to dispatch an entire cohort of intellectuals had gone awry. "The next day," Nafisi writes, "the whole of Tehran had heard the news. . . . There were many jokes about this incident."

As it happened—not in Tehran but at home in New York, and some time before coming upon Nafisi's despairing history— I had already encountered one of these jokes, as well as two of the targeted passengers. In the autumn of 1999, during an interval of thaw in the Islamic Republic's unsparing regime, a group of four

Iranian writers was permitted to depart for New York. It was a private visit, closed to the press, and presided over by an Iranian exile, the chair of a Middle Eastern department at an elite American university.* In response to an invitation from the Freedom to Write Committee of the PEN American Center, the visitors, their academic cicerone, and a pair of translators joined an attentive circle of about twenty American writers at a large round table in a small secluded room. The mood was cautious, hesitant on both sides. The Americans, conscious of their liberties in the face of writers under duress, feared giving offense by pressing too hard, and the Iranians, for their part, accustomed to wary reticence, seemed apprehensive, unsure of what unsuspected quagmires might await. But there was a prevailing good will, edged by mutual watchfulness, and the suppressed jubilation that accompanies sympathetic recognition. Here they were, these alien messengers bearing the unfathomable scars of tyranny—yet what were they really? Familiar middle-aged scribblers in shirtsleeves, worn intellectuals marked by deepening creases. You could meet their like anywhere, splitting literary hairs and grinding out cigarette butts in coffee dregs. One had a droopy Mark Twain mustache and a humorous shoulder tweaked upward by spasms of irony. He was the first to tear down the curtain of formality that shadowed the table, and it was from him that I heard the joke—it was a kind of joke—about the bus. In Iran, he said, we don't have the Rule of Law; instead we have the Rule of the Bus, mandated to pitch a score of writers over a cliff, and good riddance to critical thinking. He had spent the last twenty years, he confided, "humbly, in the corner of the kitchen"—a refuge from the despotic storm.

---

* Professor Hamid Dabashi, of Columbia University.

At the time of this visit, the despotic storm had engulfed thirteen Iranian Jews falsely accused of spying for Israel; they were charged with the sin of "world arrogance" and threatened with execution, a public iniquity that was drawing international protest and dominating the news almost daily. Only four months before, in July of 1998, another scapegoated Jew had been hanged, the most recent in a series of "anti-Zionist" persecutions. In view of the Rule of the Bus—and since hatred of "Zionists" remained a salient and enduring tenet of the ayatollahs' statecraft—it struck me as imperative not to exclude the condition of Iranian Jews in a conversation touching on human rights and free expression. The gruff and shaggy spokesman for the four, who had been introduced as "the poet of the streets," began instantly to reply in rapid Farsi. One word leaped into comprehension: *Falastin*. It was on account of the Palestinians, he explained stiffly; that was why Jews born in Isfahan were guilty. "A governmental answer," I countered, "not an answer from the corner of the kitchen." But the kitchen finally won out: the poet of the streets, it developed, had had his work banned for years, during which he earned his living writing advertising copy. He had been accused of "accepting money from Israel." He was officially a dissident. They were all dissidents; they were all secularists; they were all subject to the malevolent whims of a theocratic tyranny.

"Theocratic tyranny"—this was the Middle Eastern professor's scalding phrase. He was angry at the ayatollahs; he was angry at the fanatical influences that had corrupted a society and was punishing its intellectuals; clearly he was on the side of freedom and humanity. Yet now—startlingly, improbably—he stepped forward, bitter, strident, enraged. It was not the distant ayatollahs who were inflaming him at this hour: it was something nearer, something that was happening in this very room. The professor was white-faced. He was shouting. While an entire nation of millions is suffering under a theocratic tyranny, *you*, he scolded, are unfair, you are arrogant, to ask about thirteen Jews! Why do you pick out only the Jews to worry about? Why do they deserve separate mention?

Unfair? During the ongoing campaign against Jews, the thirteen had been selected for maltreatment in a place where, as the professor knew, the notion of judicial fairness was *Galgenhumor.* Arrogant? Surprisingly, the professor's idiom was almost identical to that of the abusive regime's typical canard of "world arrogance," employed in the usual way. And why, the American inquired, shouldn't a demographic minority—Iranian Jews—merit the same attention as the Iranian millions? Didn't the demographic minority count as *part* of those millions? Who was it really who was focusing too zealously on the Jews of Iran? Was it the objectionable American, or was it the Islamic Republic, with its nonsensical anti-Semitic inventions and its persistent cry of "Death to Israel"? Or was it, just then, the distinguished professor for whom the mere mention of Jews was an irritant?

And that is how, on November 2, 1999, the mephitic vapors of Tehran seeped, all unexpectedly, into a human rights colloquy in New York. It may be noted, though, that afterward, when the meeting was done, the man with the droopy Mark Twain mustache—the same man who had joked about the Rule of the Bus —approached the chastised American, shrugged his wry shy shrug, and smiled his tired, sensible, honest smile.

Since then, I have often thought of the man with the droopy Mark Twain mustache, and of the clandestine heroism of the corner of the kitchen. I fancy that I have met him again in Azar Nafisi's pages, where he can be fitfully glimpsed—now forcefully, now flickeringly. Nafisi calls him "my magician." His face (perhaps he is clean-shaven?) is hidden from us; how he gets his bread is left indistinct. But his principles are plain: he has succeeded in living as a free man in a brutal society. He will not accede to becoming, as Nafisi puts it, a figment of the ayatollahs' imagination. His credo is anonymity: "I want to be forgotten; I am not a member of this club. . . . In fact, I don't exist." His dissent is as absolute as it is private—and only because it is acutely private can it be absolute. Yet there is always the twisted paradox of oppression: in the ayatollahs' imagination all privacy, including the most sequestered corner of the kitchen, is transgression, and all transgression is rebellion. Hence the private individual, the invisible dissenter, is "as dangerous to the state," Nafisi concludes, "as an armed rebel."

Inspired by her magician, Nafisi herself took up arms. She and her co-conspirators—seven young women—gathered secretly on Thursday mornings in Nafisi's living room, on soft couches, over tea and cream puffs. The cream puffs and cushions are misleading: this was a war room, roiling with insurrection; the young women, arriving shrouded in their long robes and headscarves, were ardent insurgents. Their maps and weapons were at the ready—*Lolita, The Great Gatsby, Daisy Miller, Pride and Prejudice.* And also *A Thousand and One Nights*, banned in Iran and available only on the black market: the dangerously subversive Scheherazade, who knows how stories can outwit ruthlessness and confer life. That Nafisi's rebels were women is not insignificant. In the Islamic Republic, all citizens, male and female, are subject to the caprices of tyranny; but women, even as victims, are less than equal. With the ascension of Khomeini and the introduction of *sharia* law, the age of marriage for females was reduced from eighteen to nine. Stoning became the punishment for prostitution and adultery. Women were obliged to cover themselves from head to toe; to sit in the back of the bus; to avoid bright colors in coats and scarves and shoelaces. A hint of lipstick or a wayward strand of hair was likely to draw the savage solicitude of the roving moral police. Running was forbidden; licking an ice cream cone in public was forbidden; walking with a man not one's near relation was forbidden.

In her covert seminar, Nafisi's retort to these depredations was literary generalship. Her allies were Nabokov, Austen, Fitzgerald, and James—each of whom yields a powerful refraction of internal freedom and cultural despotism, of autonomy and usurpation. "The desperate truth of Lolita's story is not the rape of a twelve-year-old by a dirty old man," Nafisi argues, "but the confiscation of one individual's life by another. . . . Nabokov, through his portrayal of Humbert, had exposed all solipsists who take over other people's lives." James's Daisy Miller declines to be ruled by the expectations of her conditioning; Catherine Sloper of *Washington Square* resists not merely local convention but a deepseated drive to manipulate and subordinate her. In *Pride and Prejudice*, Nafisi points out, "there are spaces for oppositions that do not need to eliminate each other in order to exist," and it is this many-voiced disharmony—dialogue on all sides—that underlies Austen's "democratic imperative." Nafisi had come to this perception alone; but in a period of grim discouragement, reinforcement was at hand. "You used to preach to us all," her friend the magician reminded her, "that [Austen] ignored politics, not because she didn't know any better but because she didn't allow her work, her imagination, to be swallowed up by the society around her. At a time when the world was engulfed in the Napoleonic Wars, she created her own independent world, a world that you, two centuries later, in the Islamic Republic of Iran, teach as the fictional ideal of democracy. Remember all that talk of yours about how the first lesson in fighting tyranny is to . . . satisfy your own conscience?"

She remembered; she did not forget. Unlike her students, born into the ayatollahs' imperium — wherein women were legally half the value of men, and "temporary marriage," a form of sanctioned philandering, was the law — Nafisi had experienced the pre-Khomeini era. Her father had been the mayor of Tehran. Her mother had been elected to Parliament. After the Islamic revolution the two women who had been cabinet ministers were sentenced to death, "for the sins of warring with God and for spreading prostitution." The first happened to be safely abroad. The second — the former principal of Nafisi's high school — was put in a sack and stoned. Denunciations, coerced confessions, the murder of political prisoners, amputations of the limbs of thieves, show trials, and an unending procession of executions were now commonplace. The young women in Nafisi's private seminar suffered from nightmares, both in their dreams (the fear of going about unveiled) and in quotidian reality. One was allowed to attend by means of a ruse: her father believed she was translating religious texts. Another had a dictatorial husband who beat her. Still others had been jailed, or subjected to humiliatingly invasive virginity tests. Everywhere in the streets slogans on posters bawled "Death to America! Down with Imperialism and Zionism!" It was against all this that Nafisi's seven seditionists were pitted. In the conspiratorial sanctum that was Nafisi's living room, where a mirror reflected distant mountains, they threw off their somber scarves and shapeless robes and burst into an individuality of color and loosened hair. In all of Iran on a Thursday morning, it was only here that Gatsby's green light burned.

Nafisi had once been a revolutionary of a different stripe. An early marriage (it ended in divorce) took her to the University of

Oklahoma, where her then husband was studying engineering. When he returned to Iran, she stayed on, joining the demonstrations protesting the Vietnam War, "occupying" a university building, reading Lenin and Mao together with Melville and Poe. Oklahoma's Iranian students were radical Marxists. Nafisi went to their rallies, yelled their slogans, and speechified against United States support for the shah. Along the way she acquired a doctorate in literature: her dissertation was on the American proletarian novelists, exemplified by Mike Gold, the editor of *New Masses*, a 1930s periodical sympathetic to Bolshevism. Her career as a professor of literature began in the English department of the University of Tehran, just as the regime was starting its religious and political penetration of public institutions. "Almost every week, sometimes every day of the week," she recalls, "there were either demonstrations or meetings, and we were drawn to these like a magnet, independently of our will." When a popular young ayatollah, a hero of the revolution, died, rivalrous Islamic factions fought over delivering the body to its grave, while an oceanic crowd frothed in a mania of mourning and chanting. Nafisi was caught up in the communal rhapsody; she had voted for Khomeini; she had willed the revolution.

And then, as revolutions do, it swallowed her up. Vigilantes and fanatics took over. The veil was imposed on women. Books were banned. Baha'i burials were prohibited. The enemies of God multiplied; torture and executions multiplied. Nafisi's students were turning rigidly ideological. Characters in novels were judged by Islamic standards and condemned for "cultural aggression." Gatsby's Daisy was denounced as dissolute and decadent, and Gatsby was scorned as a swindler representing Western materialism. In a mordant parody that Nafisi plainly recognized — "be careful what you wish for, be careful of your dreams," she admonished one of her students, "one day they may just come true"—the ghost of the doctrinaire proletarian novel, dressed now in radical Islamic robes, rose up to haunt her: once again literature was being cut to fit prevailing dogma.

To undermine the spreading zealotry, Nafisi devised an ingenious pedagogical scheme. "This is a good time for trials," she commented dryly—her classroom would assume the trappings of a court: *The Great Gatsby* was to be put on trial. The novel would be the defendant. The students would enact judge, prosecutor, defense, and jury. Here was the prosecutor (a young man): "Imam Khomeini has relegated a great task to our poets and writers. . . . If our Imam is the shepherd who guides the flock to its pasture, then the writers are the faithful watchdogs who must lead according to the shepherd's dictates. . . . This book preaches illicit relations." And here was the defense (a young woman): "Our prosecutor has demonstrated his own weakness: an inability to read a novel on its own terms. All he knows is judgment, crude and simplistic exaltation of right and wrong. But is a novel good because the heroine is virtuous?" And now the defendant (in the voice of Nafisi): "A great novel heightens your senses and sensitivity to the complexities of life and of individuals, and prevents you from the self-righteousness that sees morality in fixed formulas about good and evil." Gatsby, the defendant insisted, is "about loss, about the perishability of dreams once they are transformed into hard reality."

At the close of the mock tribunal—a virtuoso passage in this vividly braided memoir—Nafisi appears to confront her own complicity, and that of her generation. "What we in Iran had in common with Fitzgerald," she muses, "was this dream that became our obsession and took over reality, this terrible, beautiful dream, impossible in its actualization, for which any amount of violence might be justified and forgiven." But was the dream of a politicized Islamic society, even one initially pledged to reform, ever as beautiful as it was surely terrible? When Nafisi speaks tenderly of religion, it is through her regard for her grandmother's chador, "a symbol of her sacred relationship to God. . . . It was a shelter, a world apart from the world." This serene image of pious withdrawal, an expression of inner devotion, is inescapably foreign to the bristling political belligerence of the chador under the ayatollahs' hard rule. In the falsified name of holiness thousands were arrested, movie houses were burned down, teenagers were sentenced to death, gun-toting morality squads prowled. With provocations on both sides, the eight-year war with Iraq was soon to be prosecuted. Tehran would be repeatedly bombed, and hundreds of young "martyrs," the keys to heaven swinging from their necks, would be sent to march through fields littered with land mines.

In circumstances such as these, Nafisi was expelled from the University of Tehran. She had refused to wear the veil; her refusal seemed to signify an end to teaching. She would not compromise, she could not be coerced. She entered the silenced zone of interiority, though not on the style of her friend the magician, whose principled disappearance she could not approximate. Occupied with family life, a husband and children, she was perforce in the world of common necessity. Was there, then, a middle way between compliance with the ayatollahs and the desolating seclusion of internal exile? A determined academic dynamo named Mrs. Rezvan claimed that there could be: she pressured Nafisi to take a position at Allameh Tabatabai, her "liberal" university, where, though the veil was mandatory in the classroom, Nafisi would be permitted to teach what she pleased—and besides, given that the veil was law, wasn't she already veiled when she walked out to the grocery store? A university is not a grocery, Nafisi objected; but she yielded. "Some thought I would be a traitor," she writes, "if I neglected the young and left them to the teachings of corrupt ideologies; others insisted I would be betraying everything I stood for if I worked for a regime responsible for ruining the lives of so many. . . . Both were right."

But "liberalism" in a state-controlled university was relative. The president of the faculty averted his eyes from her; religion forbade him to look at a woman. The Muslim Students Association and Islamic Jihad were active and fanatic. The walls were lined with the usual inflammatory posters. The students, constrained by beliefs and certainties that allowed no independent thought, were fearful of individuality—and it was the perplexities of individuality and autonomy that Nafisi drew from the novels her impassioned readings illumined. Jane Austen was pelted with charges of "vile," "decadent," "corrupt," the regime's hackneyed terminology. Unaccountably, there was still another source for the perversion of the aims of literature:

> One day after class, Mr. Nahvi followed me to my office. He tried to tell me that Austen was not only anti-Islamic but that she was guilty of another sin: she was a colonial writer. I was surprised to hear this from the mouth of someone who until then had mainly quoted and misquoted the Koran. He told me that *Mansfield Park* was a book that condoned slavery. . . . What confounded me was that I was almost certain that Mr. Nahvi had not read *Mansfield Park*.

Nafisi's astonishment was dispelled much later, presumably in an American academic environment, when she was introduced to the views of Edward Said; it hardly counts as a witticism to note that she was spared this particular debasement of fiction only by the intellectual isolation imposed by life under tyranny. That a Muslim fundamentalist with a circumscribed mind had gotten wind of Said's lucubrations on *Mansfield Park* suggests something about the uses of foolish ideas.

Because the intensity of the Iraqi bombings had grown unendurable, Khomeini was compelled to accept what he called the "cup of poison"—the recognition of defeat and the termination of the war. Domestic loyalties now emerged as the regime's latest motif, and again there were mass executions. Nafisi's classes expanded—strangers, students from other universities, former graduates, outsiders crowded her lectures. They came for Nabokov, for James, for Austen; they came to hear what had been taken from them. In 1989 Khomeini died. The mammoth funeral, the turbulence of the mobs, the prolonged official lamentations ignited a public frenzy comparable (though Nafisi does not tell us this) to the orgiastic obsequies surrounding Stalin's death. The ruler who was mourned as "the breaker of idols" was placed in an air-conditioned glass case. His image, it was said, could be seen in the moon. "Even perfectly modern and educated individuals came to believe this," Nafisi marvels. And Mrs. Rezvan, despite her zeal for the possibility of the liberalization of at least one Iranian university, escaped to Canada. Allameh Tabatabai had been tagged by some in the Ministry of Education as no better than Switzerland—a touchstone of Western decay.

Nafisi escaped to her living room, where her surreptitious confederates, stripped of empathy in the ayatollahs' withering domain, found it in the voices of novels, and in the safety of an intimate confessional space. Satire became the lance to pierce the hide of repressive law. Jane Austen, far from conspiring with imperialist subjugation, was, in this room of a thousand hurts, a rebel captain:

"It is a truth universally acknowledged that a Muslim man, regardless of his fortune, must be in want of a nine-year-old virgin wife." So declared Yassi, in that special tone of hers, deadpan and wildly ironic, which on some occasions, and this was one of them, bordered on the burlesque.

"Or is it a truth universally acknowledged," Manna shot back, "that a Muslim man must be in want not just of one but of many wives?"

Inexorably, the personal travail of the seven began to wash over their Thursday mornings. The social condition of women in Iran—where nail polish remained an offense worthy of flogging and prison—and the outrage of authoritarian confiscation possessed the seminar: there it was in *Lolita*, here it was in Tehran. One of Nafisi's recurrent "jokes"—not unlike the joke about the Rule of the Bus—is her account of the official censor, whose job it was to guard against insult to religion in film, theater, and television. What made him highly suitable as a judge of the visual arts was that he could not see what he condemned—he was virtually blind.

The sightless censor is Nafisi's metaphor for the Islamic Republic: it declined to see or discern. This blind callousness—Nafisi rightly terms it solipsism—ruled every cranny of the nation's existence. The answer to governmental solipsism, Nafisi determined, was insubordination through clinging to what the regime could neither see nor feel: the sympathies and openness of humane art, art freed from political manipulation—the inchoate glimmerings of Fitzgerald's green light, Nabokov's "world of tenderness, brightness and beauty," James's "Feel, feel, I say—feel for all you're worth."

But the strains of insubordination, and the tensions of oppositional thinking, could not last. "You will be leaving us soon," her friend the magician said.

She left Iran in 1997, impelled by what the great novels reveal: the right to choose. Or perhaps it was only the ayatollahs' Iran she abandoned. She kept the Iran she prized—the mountains in her living room mirror; the Persian classics, whose names, Rumi, Hafez, Sa'adi, Khayyam, Nezami, Ferdowsi, Attar, Beyhaghi, are an elixir of language; the memory of her underground magician, on whose repudiations civilization finally depends.

In Iran, until recently, the straits of courage through which one might pass with conscience nearly unscathed seemed few. The magician's way: I am not a member of this club. Mrs. Rezvan's way: why deprive the young of what they deserve to have, and only you can give?—which led first to compromise and then to disillusionment. And last, emigration, whenever it proved feasible, and if not, then through the connivance of smugglers. The Rule of the Bus rendered any other solution unthinkable.

Yet lately, especially among the young, there are rumblings of cracks in the ayatollahs' regime. A fore-echo was heard even before Nafisi's departure, when a former student, no longer wearing the chador, confided that she had named her child Daisy: "I want my daughter to be what I never was." Once an ideologically indignant adherent of the Muslim Students Association, she had resisted Nafisi's charge that a novel is "not an exercise in censure." She had admired a professor who erased the impious word "wine" from his readings. And she had emphatically assailed James's Daisy as licentious. "As I write," Nafisi notes in her epilogue, "I open the paper to read about the student demonstrations in support of a dissident who was sentenced to death for suggesting that the clergy should not be blindly followed like monkeys."

And as I write, in the summer of 2003, I open the paper to read of student protests in Tehran—the burning of tires, the burning of trees—directed against Khamenei, the current ruling ayatollah, and also against President Khatami, the designated reformist figure. (When Khatami appeared on American television some months past, it was all a matter of Tweedledum and Tweedledee.*) Twenty-four years ago, the students of the Islamic revolution were chanting "Death to America." Now their sons and daughters are chanting "Death to Khamenei, kill all the mullahs," and still the tune is death. A generation has been reared on death —death as justice, death as retribution, death as religion, death as victory, death as intoxication. Revolutions are rarely velvet, and most often cannot be, especially when sanctified thugs and their truncheons come calling—but death-yelps as the birth pangs of democracy?

Nafisi's anguished and glorious memoir contemplates another theme: "how fragile is his life," she thinks, visiting her magician for the last time. She is with him in the corner of the kitchen, imagining the future. She will go on reading *Lolita* in the United States. He will stay behind. How much more promising it would be if the beleaguered summoners of a world yet unborn were moved to cry "Long life to Sheherazade!" in the streets of Tehran.

---

* And how much more so in the summer of 2005, when Mahmoud Ahmadinejad, Iran's newly elected president, an Islamic hard-liner, was said to have been recognized by his former American captives as one of the hostage takers who seized the U.S. embassy in Tehran in November 1979.

Isaac Babel:
"Let Me Finish"

§ On May 15, 1939, Isaac Babel, a writer whose distinction had earned him the Soviet privilege of a villa in the country, was arrested at Peredelkino and taken to Moscow's Lubyanka prison, headquarters of the secret police. His papers were confiscated and destroyed—among them half-completed stories, plays, film scripts, translations. Six months later, after three days and nights of hellish interrogation, he confessed to a false charge of espionage. The following year, a clandestine trial was briefly held in the dying hours of January 25; Babel recanted his confession, appealed to his innocence, and at 1:40 the next morning was summarily shot by a firing squad. He was forty-five. His final plea was not for himself, but for the power and truth of literature: "Let me finish my work."

What Kafka's art hallucinates—trial without cause, an inescapable predicament directed by an irrational force, a malignant social order—Babel is at last condemned to endure in the living flesh. Kafka and Babel can be said to be the twentieth century's European coordinates: they are separated by language, style, and temperament; but where their fevers intersect lies the point of infection. Each was an acutely conscious Jew. Each witnessed a pogrom while still very young, Kafka in enlightened Prague, Babel under a czarist regime that promoted harsh legal disabilities for Jews. Each invented a type of literary modernism, becoming a movement in himself, with no possibility of successors. To be influenced by Kafka is to end in parody; and because the wilderness of an astoundingly variegated experience is incised, unduplicatably, in the sinews of Babel's prose, no writer can effectively claim to be his disciple.

But of course they are opposites: Kafka ingrown, self-dissatisfied, indifferent to politics; hardly daring, despite genius, to feel entitlement to his own language; endlessly agonizing over a broken engagement; rarely leaving home. And here is Babel, insouciant, reckless, a womanizer, half a vagabond, a horseman, a propagandist, the father of three by three different women, only one of them legally his wife. Then why bring up Kafka when speaking of Babel? Kafka at least died in his bed. Babel was murdered by the criminal agency of a cynically criminal government. Kafka requested that his writing be destroyed, and was not obeyed. Babel's name and work were erased—as if he had never written at all—until 1954, when, during a "thaw," he was, in Soviet terminology, rehabilitated.

Yet taken together, they tell us what we in our time are obliged to know about the brutal tracings of force and deception, including self-deception. Kafka alone is not enough; his interiors are too circumscribed. Babel alone is not enough; his landscapes are too diffuse. Kafka supplies the grandly exegetical metaphor: the man who thinks but barely lives, the metaphysician who is ultimately consumed by a conflagration of lies. Babel, by contrast, lives, lives, lives! He lives robustly, inquisitively, hungrily; his appetite for unpredictable human impulse is gargantuan, inclusive, eccentric. He is trickster, rapscallion, ironist, wayward lover, imprudent impostor —and out of these hundred fiery selves insidious truths creep out, one by one, in a face, in the color of the sky, in a patch of mud, in a word. Violence, pity, comedy, illumination. It is as if he is an irritable membrane, subject to every creaturely vibration.

He was born in Odessa, a cosmopolitan and polyglot city that looked to the sea and beyond. It was, he wrote,

> the most charming city of the Russian Empire. If you think about it, it is a town in which you can live free and easy. Half the population is made up of Jews, and Jews are a people who have learned a few simple truths along the way. Jews get married so as not to be alone, love so as to live through the centuries, save money so they can buy houses and give their wives astrakhan jackets, love children because, let's face it, it is good and important to love one's children. The poor Odessa Jews get very confused when it comes to officials and regulations, but it isn't all that easy to get them to budge in their opinions, their very antiquated opinions. You might not be able to budge these Jews, but there's a whole lot you can learn from them. To a large extent it is because of them that Odessa has this light and easy atmosphere.

There is much of the affectionate and mirthful Babel in this paragraph: the honest yet ironic delight in people exactly as they are, the teasing sense of laughing entitlement ("so as to live through the centuries"), prosperity and poverty rubbing elbows, ordinary folk harried by officialdom, confusion and stubbornness, love and loneliness. As for poor Jews, Babel began as one of these, starting life in the Moldavanka, a mixed neighborhood with a sprinkling of mobsters. What he witnessed there, with a bright boy's perceptiveness, catapulted him early on into the capacious worldliness that burst out (he was twenty-nine) in the exuberant tales of Benya Krik and his gang—tough but honorable criminals with a Damon Runyonesque strain.

Lionel Trilling, among the first to write seriously about Babel in English, mistook him for "a Jew of the ghetto." If "ghetto" implies a narrow and inbred psyche, then Babel stands for the reverse. Though he was at home in Yiddish and Hebrew, and was familiar with the traditional texts and their demanding commentaries, he added to these a lifelong infatuation with Maupassant and Flaubert. His first stories were composed in fluent literary French. The breadth and scope of his social compass enabled him to see through the eyes of peasants, soldiers, priests, rabbis, children, artists, actors, women of all classes. He befriended whores, cab drivers, jockeys; he knew what it was to be penniless, to live on the edge and off the beaten track. He was at once a poet of the city—"the glass sun of Petersburg"—and a lyricist of the countryside: "the walls of sunset collapsing into the sky." He was drawn to spaciousness and elasticity, optimism and opportunity, and it was through these visionary seductions of societal freedom, expressed politically, that he welcomed the Revolution.

He not only welcomed it; he joined it. In order to be near Maxim Gorky, his literary hero, Babel had been living illegally in St. Petersburg, one of the cities prohibited to Jews under the hobbling restrictions of the czarist Pale of Settlement. With the advent of the Revolution the Pale dissolved, discriminatory quotas ceased, censorship vanished, promises multiplied, and Babel zealously attached himself to the Bolshevik cause. In 1920, as a war correspondent riding with the Red Cavalry to deliver Communist salvation to the reluctant Polish villages across the border, he fell into disenchantment. "They all say they're fighting for justice and they all loot," he wrote in his diary. "Murderers, it's unbearable, baseness and crime. . . . Carnage. The military commander and I ride along the tracks, begging the men not to butcher the prisoners." Six years later, Babel published his penetratingly authoritative *Red Cavalry* stories, coolly steeped in pity and blood, and found instant fame.

With Stalin's ascension in 1924, new tyrannies began to

mimic the old. Postrevolutionary literary and artistic ferment, much of it experimental, ebbed or was suppressed. Censorship returned, sniffing after the subversive, favoring the coarse flatness of Socialist Realism. Babel's wife, Evgenia, whom he had married in 1919, emigrated to Paris, where his daughter Nathalie was born in 1929. His mother and sister, also disaffected, left for Brussels. Babel clung to Moscow, hotly wed to his truest bride, the Russian tongue, continuing his work on a cycle of childhood stories and venturing into writing for theater and film. The film scripts, especially those designed for silent movies, turned out to be remarkable: they took on, under the irresistible magnetism of the witnessing camera and the innovation of the present tense, all the surreal splendor of Babel's most plumaged prose. Several were produced and proved to be popular, but eventually they failed to meet Party guidelines, and the director of one of them, an adaptation of Turgenev, was compelled to apologize publicly.

Unable to conform to official prescriptiveness, Babel's publications grew fewer and fewer. He was charged with "silence"—the sin of Soviet unproductivity—and was denied the privilege of traveling abroad. His last journey to Paris occurred in 1935, when André Malraux intervened with the Soviet authorities to urge Babel's attendance at a Communist-sponsored International Congress of Writers for the Defense of Culture and Peace—after which Babel never again met with his wife and daughter. Later that year, back in Moscow, he set up a second household with Antonina Pirozhkova, with whom he fathered a second daughter; through an earlier liaison, he was already the father of a son. But if Babel's personal life was unpredictable, disorganized, and rash, his art was otherwise. He wrested his sentences out of a purifying immediacy. Like Pushkin, he said, he was in pursuit of "precision and brevity." His most pointed comment on literary style appears in "Guy de Maupassant," a cunning seriocomic sexual fable fixed on the weight and trajectory of language itself. The success of a phrase, the young narrator instructs, "rests in a crux that is barely discernible. One's fingertips must grasp the key, gently warming it. And then the key must be turned once, not twice." But even this is not the crux. The crux (Babel's severest literary dictum) is here: "No iron spike can pierce a human heart as icily as a period in the right place."

A writer's credo, and Babel's most intimate confession. Stand in awe of it, yes—but remember also that this same master of the white bone of truth, this artist of the delicately turned key, was once a shameless propagandist for the Revolution, capable of rabid rote exhortations: "Beat them, Red Fighters, clobber them to death, if it is the last thing you do! Right away! This minute! Now!" "Slaughter them, Red Army fighters! Stamp harder on the rising lids of their rancid coffins!" Such catchwords are locked cells for which there are no keys, and while it is a truism that every utopia contains the seeds of dystopia, Babel, after all, was granted skepticism almost from the start. Out of skepticism came disillusionment; out of disillusionment, revulsion. And in the end, as the tragic trope has it, the Revolution devoured its child.

Babel's art served as a way station to the devouring. He was devoured because he would not, could not, accommodate to falsehood; because he saw and he saw, with an eye as merciless as a klieg light; and because, like Kafka, he surrendered his stories to voices and passions tremulous with the unforeseen. If we wish to complete, and transmit, the literary configuration of the twentieth century—the image that will enduringly stain history's retina —now is the time (it is past time) to set Babel beside Kafka. Between them, they leave no nerve unshaken.

In Research
of Lost Time

§ "I'M A REPORTER, not a biographer," Joseph Lelyveld warns in an early passage of *Omaha Blues*, his distinctly reportorial memoir. This insistently honest assertion is confirmed by Lelyveld's history of hierarchical ascent at the *New York Times*: from errand boy (a daily run to the Weather Bureau) to local and national newshawk, to foreign correspondent, and eventually to executive editor. Retired now from the pinnacle of a long career, he has sought in his late sixties to mine the partly veiled, partly relinquished landscape of an irregular childhood. And it is as a seasoned journalist—legman, interviewer, researcher, chaser after leads—that he goes about the often harrowing job of uncovering painful old family truths. His is the restrained newspaperman's voice of principled detachment: no taking sides, little introspection, narrative plumbed for data and evidence rather than motive or metaphor.

But the data are mostly tumultuous, and the evidence turns out to be as ambiguous as it is troubling. Memory itself, frail and dappled, is scarcely trustworthy, and is anyhow the poet's tool; yet Lelyveld means to reconstruct—no, to reanimate—the faded lives and hidden passions of his parents, and of Ben, an enigmatic older friend: the central trio of his boyhood. Self-defined as a "scavenger of archives," he plunges into the documented sources. He requests FBI files of half a century ago. He looks up court records, defunct newspapers, film libraries, historical societies, the relics of disbanded committees. He tracks down a schoolmate he has not spoken to since the ninth grade. He excavates an old trunk stuffed with letters and stored in a synagogue basement. And in this way he hopes to retrieve the dramatis personae of an unhappy childhood: father, mother, Ben.

Each was a force, and ultimately an absence. His father, Arthur Lelyveld, was an eminent Reform rabbi and a committed civil rights activist. From the pulpit of his Cleveland synagogue he pressed for the integration of that city's public schools. In the "freedom summer" of 1964 he was brutally beaten and bloodied with a tire iron by racist thugs in Mississippi. But twenty years earlier, in the heart of the Second World War, in the very hour when the fires of Auschwitz were obliterating the Jews of Europe, a misplaced pacifist zeal had led him to a position acutely grotesque for a Jewish leader. Idealist purity took on a problematical, even a chimerical, taint: he proposed to send a Jewish "relief unit" to Europe, to be composed of conscientious objectors like himself. However respectful of human life and unwilling to shed blood he might be, a conscientious objector in that period was nevertheless a bystander to the murder of Jews.

Delusion evaporated finally in the blaze of intelligent hindsight, and Arthur Lelyveld became a tireless advocate for the Zionist cause, at first working to bring round Jews inimical to the idea of Jewish nationhood. Prominent among these was Arthur Hays Sulzberger, the publisher of the *New York Times*; Sulzberger was not won over. At thirty-three, Arthur Lelyveld joined a delegation to the Oval Office to plead with an irritable Truman for the establishment of the Jewish state. "Jesus Christ couldn't please them when he was on earth," the president was reported to have said. Still, Joseph recalls, "my dad came home thinking he had made a sale."

Joseph's mother, meanwhile, was an idealist of a different color. Though at twenty-one she had begun her marriage with radiant visions of a midwestern clerical life, she soon discovered that the role of *rebbetzin*, the rabbi's wife, was far too restrictive for her emerging literary and scholarly ambitions. In her teens she had performed in amateur theatricals, and continued to be drawn to drama: the year Joseph was born she was directing a play by Clifford Odets. Increasingly restless, she wearied of her duties as a purveyor of congregational politesse. What she craved was Shakespeare and doctoral study at Columbia University with Maurice Valency, a popular Renaissance scholar and drama consultant. "I'm in a world I adore," she wrote from Morningside Heights, having left behind both husband and two small sons.

In 1943, nine-year-old Joseph (stylishly dubbed Jo by his mother, after the sculptor Jo Davidson) abruptly became Joey in mud-soaked rural Tekamah, north of Omaha, where his father then held his pulpit. The boy was uprooted—farmed out, literally—and sent to live with the Jensens, a Seventh-day Adventist family. The Sabbatarian Jensens shunned pork; the Reform Lelyvelds did not. On the Jensens' 240-acre farm Joey milked cows, put up wallpaper to thwart leaks, and learned that "cultivatin" meant "diggin out the pig weeds." Both Lelyveld parents were distantly preoccupied with their divided aspirations, the father looking to succor the world's forlorn, the mother in New York, intellectually liberated from domesticity and resentful of its claims. Despite love poems and pleas from her husband, she declined to return to him. Joseph was again shipped off, this time to Brooklyn and the care of his paternal grandparents. Torn between the divergent urgencies of traditional wifehood and the seductions of Shakespeare, his mother suffered repeated breakdowns; there were three suicide attempts.

But there were also repeated reconciliations, during one of which Michael, Joseph's youngest brother, was born. In a clan of blonds, Michael was dark-haired. His actual father, it was revealed long afterward, was Maurice Valency. And still the marriage lasted, even in the face of multiple stormy separations, for some thirty years. This did not prevent Joseph from fathoming, early on, that as a child of intermittent parents he was to be dismissed as secondary to their respective primary passions.

Enter Ben, Joseph's affectionate and attentive grown-up pal. Like Arthur Lelyveld, he too was a rabbi; he had been ordained as a graduate of the first class of the Jewish Institute of Religion, a new seminary founded by the renowned Rabbi Stephen S. Wise, a friend of Woodrow Wilson and the nation's foremost Zionist spokesman. Unlike Joseph's often unavailable father, Ben was open to the confidences of an otherwise stubbornly reticent boy, and willingly shepherded him to innumerable baseball games. Yet much of Ben's background was strangely shrouded. Was he or wasn't he a Communist, or even a Soviet agent? Hadn't he consorted with Vasily Zarubin, the KGB's man in the United States, who had twice been awarded the Order of Lenin, and whose spies had penetrated the Manhattan Project? The FBI had all along been collecting observations mixed with suspicions concerning one Benjamin Lowell, who had been George B. Stern, who had been Rabbi Benjamin Goldstein of Temple Beth Or in Montgomery, Alabama.

Temple Beth Or was Ben's first pulpit. He preached against the wretchedly low wages paid to workers in the South. He preached on the "Negro question." When the Scottsboro Boys, nine young black men falsely accused of raping two white women, were confined on death row in a Montgomery jail, Ben was the only white clergyman to visit them. Together with local black ministers, he organized protest rallies on their behalf, and defended their innocence in a Yom Kippur sermon. His congregants trembled; in rigidly stratified Montgomery, they were themselves insecure. The mayor of Montgomery, it was said, had warned of boycotts of Jewish businesses, and possible violence by the Klan. The Beth Or board ordered Ben to "desist doing anything further in the Scottsboro case." Ousted from his position and charged with Communist connections, Ben was effectively run out of town.

Rabbi Wise, his mentor, into whose family he had married, offered less than tepid support: Ben's name was turning up in one Communist front organization after another. Now known as George B. Stern, he had drifted off to Hollywood, where he was working for a company that distributed Soviet films. In 1939, in an outrageously sloganeering letter to Rabbi Wise, he made excuses justifying the Nazi-Soviet Pact. "The high, holy peace of the Nazi and Communist saints," Wise wrote back bitterly.

But when the young Joseph Lelyveld met a captivating Ben in the summer of 1948, the paramount subject was baseball, and Ben himself was now styled Rabbi Benjamin B. Lowell (a WASPized name swiped from his second wife, née Lowenstein). He had been hired as an assistant to Arthur Lelyveld, who was then directing the Hillel Foundation, a nationwide Jewish campus society. "For a couple of years," Lelyveld writes, "Ben was the one adult in my life who seemed consistently and reliably available. . . . I'd never felt as indulged as I did in Ben's company."

This may account for Ben's powerfully disproportionate presence in these pages. The mammoth archival effort Lelyveld expends on Ben is, after all, neither the measure nor the essence of the boy's need. The boy knows nothing of Ben's political life. It is for his indulgence, not his politics, that Ben is cherished. The political Ben, the Soviet-apologist Ben, is beyond the boy's scope or interest; if he dominates, it is because of the scope and interest of the journalist. *Omaha Blues* is subtitled "A Memory Loop." But the Ben who takes over and sets the tone of this narrative is only partly in Lelyveld's memory loop. He is preeminently in Lelyveld's research loop—which is why Ben's every affiliation with all manner of Communist fronts is sumptuously explored. Having recovered that 1939 letter to Stephen Wise, Ben's brash pronunciamento that the Soviet Union is not "on the side of the despisers of mankind," Lelyveld sighs, "Oh Ben"—the impatient despair of the mature political reporter immersed in the unsavory events of the 1930s and 1940s. "I can only be grateful," he adds, "the archives haven't yielded my old friend's rationalization for the Moscow trials." Here speaks the editorialist; the hurt boy is forgotten, fallen out of the memory loop. The blues are muted.

For the hurt boy, Ben was for a time a "solid presence." Then he disappeared—another instance of an inconstant world. He disappeared because Joseph's father sacked him. Though Arthur Lelyveld had resisted the prevailing pressures of redbaiting, he finally lost confidence in his deputy. The Korean War was under way, and Ben had been fundraising at a front meeting where America was accused of manipulating the United Nations on behalf of a reactionary regime. "The former pacifist," Lelyveld reflects, "had to ask his assistant how on earth . . . he could mindlessly fall in step with a cynical peace campaign designed in Moscow, a throwback to the era of the Nazi-Soviet Pact when believers like Ben learned to denounce 'the second imperialist war.'" For fifteen years Ben had not veered from the party line. The Marshall Plan, he once remarked, was an American capitalist plot to seize Europe's markets. Sadly, "Ben had put [my dad] in a situation where he ended up closer to the position of the witch-hunters than he ever imagined he could find himself. It was Ben who had stuck him there, sure, but then what's freedom of speech for if it only belongs to those who'll always be beyond reproach in the use they make of it?"

This last sentiment is unexceptionable, but once again it has an editorial ring. A more contentious, or call it loyalist, declaration crops up elsewhere. In an extraordinary irony of the generations, the Zionist rabbi and his journalist son were destined to parody history by trading places. "One of my father's tasks as a Zionist official," Lelyveld writes in a footnote, "was to try to persuade the *Times* that it was giving the anti-Zionist position excessive coverage. He never got to meet the publisher but periodically called on Sulzberger's second-in-command, Julius Ochs Adler." Years later, here is Lelyveld standing in Adler's stead, fending off "a rabbi in full cry who accused the *Times* of using its news columns with malice aforethought to undermine Israel." Critical views like these Lelyveld dismisses as "Jewish folk belief."

The complainer in question, however, was a member of the Central Conference of American Rabbis, of which, as it happened, Arthur Lelyveld was president. Learning of this incident, Lelyveld tells us, his father sighed the familial Lelyveld sigh, "a tic passed from generation to generation," and "offered no comment. He understood that the approaches of an advocate and a journalist had to differ." Possibly this was the very argument with which Adler had long ago sent Lelyveld's father packing. Its hidden flaw is that it will sometimes, under the banner of high principle, preclude useful corrective self-interrogation. Did the senior Lelyveld's sigh signify that vaunted neutrality may on occasion be tantamount to evasiveness?

The approaches of a memoirist and a journalist can also be

said to differ. Or put it that there is no all-pervading Proustian madeleine in Lelyveld's workaday prose. Yet salted through this short work is the smarting of an unpretentious lamentation: "If this were a novel," "If I were using these events in a novel," and so on. Flickeringly, the writer appears to see what is missing; and what is missing is the intuitive, the metaphoric, the uncertain, the introspective with its untethered vagaries: in brief, the not-nailed-down. Consequently Lelyveld's memory loop becomes a memory hole, through which everything that is not factually retrievable escapes. Memory, at bottom, is an act of imaginative re-creation, not of archival legwork. "Yes, I was finding, it was possible to do a reporting job on your childhood," Lelyveld insists. Yes? Perhaps no. The memoirist has this in common with the novelist: he is like the watchful spider alert to every quiver on its lines. Sensation, not research. Even the conflicted interlude on the farm is retraced (but not replenished) through informational interviews and correspondence, not through the child's sense of desertion and loss. It is telling that what Lelyveld terms "a transfixing moment" of his adolescence turns on an ideological debate with a Communist schoolmate.

All the same, there are three genuinely transfixing moments —infusions of transcendence—that take this markedly political mindset by surprise. Assigned in 1976 to a presidential campaign in Omaha, Lelyveld visits a transient site of his childhood, the house that is now an institution for the troubled young. "The deep closet of my parents' bedroom" he remembers as a luring tunnel leading to a heap of *National Geographic* magazines; the laundry sink in the basement calls up "thoughts of model planes." Here, suddenly, is the heat of flesh and blood: intimations of the living thinking feeling boy, and what he read, and the thrilling smells of balsawood and glue. (And here Lelyveld himself scents the revelatory madeleine.)

Next, reproduced on the page in black and white, without a caption, a rather amateurish watercolor of his mother, painted by a family friend, and belatedly plucked from the synagogue trunk. A woman sunk in discontent, beautiful, longing, pensive, unsayably sad.

And last, a vision of himself that came upon the fifty-nine-year-old Lelyveld in the course of his father's funeral, even as the eulogies thickened: "I imagined a little boy with curly blond hair . . . running up a slight slope, through high grass, on a summery day. The little boy was calling, 'Daddy, Daddy, Daddy . . .'"

The closet, the sink, the portrait, the cry of "Daddy" weigh more in this uneasy history of a childhood than the documents, interviews, letters, political trackings, and all the reportorial rest.

The Heretical Passions
of Gershom Scholem

$\oint$ O N E   M O R N I N G   E A R L Y   in February, 1917, Gerhard Scholem, a very tall, jug-eared, acutely bookish young man of nineteen, sat at breakfast with his parents in their comfortable Berlin apartment. It was an hour of family crisis. Gerhard, the youngest of four sons, was the only one still living at home. The three others had all been conscripted for the kaiser's war. Reinhold and Erich were solid German patriots like their father; Reinhold went so far as to call himself, in right-wing lingo, a *Deutschnationaler*—a German nationalist. Werner, Gerhard's senior by two years, was a hothead and a leftist—he would later become a committed Communist. He had been wounded in the foot in the Serbian campaign and was recuperating in an army hospital. Limping, wearing his uniform, he abandoned his bed and made his way to an antiwar demonstration. He was arrested and charged with treason.

Over the uneaten pastries, yet another brand of treason was brewing. Gerhard had declared himself to be a Zionist, and was openly preparing for emigration to Palestine. Two years earlier, exposed as the author of an antiwar flyer circulated by a Zionist youth group, he had been expelled from high school. Arthur Scholem, the paterfamilias of this opinionated crew (half of them mutinous), could do nothing about Werner, who was in the hands of the military. But Gerhard was near enough to feel his father's rage, and Arthur Scholem had devised a punishment of Prussian thoroughness. Demanding, authoritarian, uncompromising, practical above all, he was the kind of father we have met before: Kafka's notoriously uncomprehending father, say, or T. S. Eliot's father, a brick manufacturer for whom poets were idlers. Like these stern pragmatists, Arthur Scholem was a businessman; he presided over a successful printing enterprise and a household that could keep both a cook and a maid. At Christmas there was an elaborately decorated tree, surrounded by heaps of presents. When Gerhard was fourteen, he found under the tree a framed portrait of Theodor Herzl, the founder of modern Zionism. "We selected this picture for you because you are so interested in Zionism," his mother explained. ("From then on," Scholem commented decades later, "I left the house at Christmastime.")

This interest, in Arthur Scholem's view, had increasingly turned excessive and unreasonable. Gerhard had not only hurled himself obsessively into the study of Hebrew; he was entering, with the identical zeal he gave to Latin and German literature, the capacious universe of the Talmud, that oceanic compilation of interpretive biblical commentaries. Every element of these ancient canonical texts attracted him—their ethical and jurisprudential preoccupations; the vitality, in equal measure, of their rational and imaginative insights; their famous argumentativeness and inclusiveness; their dialogical and often dissenting discourse across the generations. The romanticized work of Martin Buber and Heinrich Graetz's panoramic *History of the Jews* (both of which Scholem eventually took issue with) were the initial stimuli, but he went on to search out the Zionist theoreticians of the time, and anything in Judaica that a bibliomaniacal teenage boy haunting secondhand bookshops could afford.

All this was too much for the elder Scholem—who routinely paid dues, after all, to the vehemently anti-Zionist Central Association of German Citizens of the Jewish Faith. The faith might be tepidly Jewish; the primary allegiance—the unquestioned identity, both social and personal—was German. Arthur Scholem believed himself to be an established and accepted member of a stable society. But Werner was a Marxist and Gerhard a Zionist—two sons out of four dangerously dreaming of new worlds yet unborn. No wonder "the discussions at the family table became heated," as Scholem wryly points out in *From Berlin to Jerusalem*, his concise little memoir of 1977. But by then Gerhard had long since been transmuted into Gershom.

On that February morning in 1917, the family table was less heated than quietly tense. Arthur Scholem had made his preparations; he waited. The doorbell rang, heralding the arrival of a registered letter. It had been composed two nights earlier, and was addressed to Gerhard:

> I have decided to cut off all support to you. Bear in mind the following: you have until the first of March to leave my house, and you will be forbidden to enter it again without my permission. On March first, I will transfer 100 marks to your account so that you will not be left without means. Anything more than this you cannot expect from me. . . . Whether I will agree to finance your further studies after the war depends upon your future behavior.
>
> Your father, Arthur Scholem

The father's misunderstanding was absolute. He could not fathom a young man opposed to a patriotic war. Having a prodigy on his hands bewildered him—a rebellious prodigy given to devouring Plato and Kant, uncommonly gifted in higher mathematics, and determined to add to this conceptual stew an unfashionable, unpredictable, altogether obstinate dedication to Jewish history and thought. And beyond these perplexities, Arthur Scholem scarcely recognized what Gerhard, in choosing to become Gershom (the name of a son of the biblical Moses), was crucially repudiating—and would continue to repudiate for the rest of his life. Despite Scholem's own mastery of European culture, it was Europe, and Germany in particular, he meant to renounce. His father's loyalties—the passionately held love of the *Vaterland* that the majority of German Jews plainly felt—he could see only as self-deception. The Jews might be in love with Germany, but Germany was not in love with the Jews. To a Jewish friend who had professed "boundless adoration for German art, Goethe, and our contemporary Richard Borchardt," and who provocatively added, "I hate Martin Buber with all my heart," the nineteen-year-old Scholem responded with what he called "a tremendous intuition" for Judaism:

> I confess that I've never had such a central relationship with any other thing; it has commanded my full attention from the time I began to work and think for myself (to wit, from the age of fourteen). The confrontation with German culture which presents so many Jews with such painful dilemmas has never been a problem for me. Nor has the absolutely non-Jewish atmosphere in my home been able to change this. I have never found or sought out values whose legitimacy was rooted in the German essence. Even the German language, which I speak, disappears for me completely when compared to Hebrew.

To another correspondent, a few days before, he had announced, "We [Jews] have had a relationship with Europe only to the degree that Europe has acted on us as a destructive stimulation." Both these assertions were made from a bed in a military hospital, where, he reported, "the heavy footsteps of anti-Semitism are always thumping behind my back." Like his older brothers before him, he had been drafted; unlike Werner, he had not been wounded in battle. He was, instead, in a mental ward, suffering from a kind of nervous disorder—and then again it was an invention, "a colossal fabrication," as he put it, to get himself out of the army. In fact it was partly one and partly the other, and it succeeded in freeing him. "I'll be able to work again," he crowed. "I won't be squandering my youth in these odious circumstances, and I can celebrate my twentieth birthday wearing civilian clothes."

The three-month interval between his father's throwing him out of the house and his induction into the military had turned out to be remarkably fruitful. He went to live at the Pension Struck, a boarding house in an unfashionable neighborhood of Berlin catering to a group of Russian-Jewish intellectuals who held perfervid, if conflicting, Zionist views. Among the polyglot and fiercely literary boarders was a future president of Israel, and it was here that Scholem undertook a translation from the Yiddish (a language new to him) of a volume of memorial essays devoted to Jewish victims of Arab rioters in Palestine: his first full-length publication. During this same period he began his enduring friendship with the Hebrew novelist S. Y. Agnon, who would one day be awarded the Nobel Prize in Literature, and whose stories Scholem rendered into pellucid German. Scholem had already encountered Walter Benjamin at a Jewish discussion club for young people—"an utterly original mind," he marveled. He was then sixteen; Benjamin was five years older. Not long afterward they met again, as university students. (Despite

Scholem's expulsion from high school, he was permitted to take his graduation exams and managed to gain university entrance through an academic loophole intended for Junkers.) The two talked of phenomenology and philology; they talked of socialism and historiography; they talked of Chinese philosophy and of Baudelaire, Pindar, and Hölderlin; they argued over Brecht and Zola and Zionism; they were mutually immersed in Kafka. These astonishing exchanges—the bulk of them through a decades-long correspondence indefatigably pledged to ideas, experimental, often playful, and on Benjamin's part somewhat elusive—continued until Benjamin's suicide in 1940, in flight from the Germans. Scholem was frequently the first reader of Benjamin's newest work, and Benjamin was briefly inspired by Scholem's example to study Hebrew, though he never progressed much beyond the alphabet. It was an intimacy rooted in mind. Both of these extraordinary young men were beguiled by the transcendent nature of language. Both were out to recreate intellectual history—Benjamin with the uncertainty of his genius, wavering from subject to subject, Scholem with the certainty of his, leaping with scholarly ferocity into the hitherto untouchable cauldron of Jewish mysticism.

It was untouchable because it was far out of the mainstream of Judaism, excluded by rabbinic consensus. Normative Judaism saw itself as given over to moral rationalism: to codes of ethics, compassionate conduct, including the primacy of charity, and a coherent set of personal and societal practices; to the illuminations of Midrash, the charms of ethical lore—but mythologies and esoteric mysteries were cast out. Mysticism was regarded as waywardness, and notions of divine immanence seemed too perilously close to paganism. The *Zohar*, a mystical treatise, was grudgingly admitted for study, but only in maturity, lest it dazzle the student into irrationality. For normative Judaism, ripe sobriety was all; or, if not all, then a significant social ideal.

Scholem saw something else, and he saw it from an early age. Unlike Freud, who dismissed religion as illusion, Scholem more ambitiously—more penetratingly—believed it to be as crucial for the structure of the human mind as language itself. At twenty-one he wrote to Escha Burckhardt (whom he would later marry and divorce), "Philology is truly a secret science and the only legitimate form of historical science that has existed until now. It is the greatest confirmation of my view of the central importance of Tradition, though of course in a new sense of the word." He named his idea "the philosophy of the Hebrew language" and exclaimed, prophetically, "Oh, if only some day these things could be the focus of my worthy labors!" This ardent cry was more than an inkling or a premonition; it was the annunciation of precocious self-knowledge.

Two years on, he was a doctoral student who described his dissertation as "a vast foundational philological-philosophical monograph on an early kabbalistic text from around the year 1230. . . . Nothing worthwhile that's any longer than four pages has been written about it." His work on this text, *Sefer ha-Bahir*, was pioneering scholarship, but it was far more than that. In the framework of conventional Jewish historiography it signaled a revolution. Scholem was uncovering a tradition hidden underneath, and parallel to, normative Jewish religious expression. Below the ocean of interpretive commentary lay another ocean, also of interpretive commentary, but in imagistic and esoteric guise: "a strictly monotheistic form of gnosticism," Scholem called it, "according to which the God of Israel is the true God of the mystics." (Pagan and Christian Gnosticism posited an antagonistic duality: the false Creator-God of the Jews, and the covert true

God.) Scholem's encyclopedic research took him through the centuries; no one before him had ever systematically ordered and investigated the manifold varieties of Jewish mysticism. The position of classical Judaism was that the essence of God is unknowable: "Thou canst not see My Face." The Kabbalists sought not only to define and characterize the Godhead—through a kind of spiritualized cosmogonic physics—but to experience it. Kabbalah had been rabbinically shunned for its claims of ecstatic ascent to the hidden sublime; it had been rabbinically scorned for its connection to folk religion and magic. Scholem himself was unapologetic in confronting the lower forms of Kabbalistic practice. "In this descent from the heights of theosophical speculation to the depths of popular thought and action," he acknowledged,

> the ideas of the Kabbalists undoubtedly lost much of their radiance. In their concrete embodiment they often became crude. The dangers with which myth and magic threaten the religious mind are exemplified in the history of Judaism by the development of Kabbalah, and anyone who concerns himself seriously with the thinking of the great Kabbalists will be torn between feelings of admiration and revulsion.

Revulsion might be inspired by such ritualized acts of magic as "putting on the Name," a fourteenth-century ceremony whereby a sleeveless garment made of deerskin parchment is inscribed with the secret names of God. After donning this, and a cap to match, and invoking the help of angels, the adept is obliged to fast for seven days, following which he calls out the divine Name over a body of water. If a green shape rises up, he is judged unclean and must repeat his fast, along with giving alms. But if the apparition emerges as red, he is purified, and may enter the water up to his loins—the climax of an initiation said to clothe him in formidable otherworldly strength.

Yet despite these degraded theurgic usages, Scholem was determined to pry the loftier facets of a suppressed mystical tradition from their concealment, partly to complete and clarify the historical record, and partly to disclose arcane and majestic imaginative constructs, themselves marvels of human intellect. It was a kind of literary archaeology. His chief excavating tool was philology—the study of texts and their origins. Scholem has been compared to one of the greatest of the grand exegetes and codifiers of Jewish tradition—Maimonides, the twelfth-century physician and polymath, who read Torah with an Aristotelian eye. But Maimonides was a proponent of rationalism. Scholem was in pursuit of the opposite. He looked to theosophy, as manifested in Kabbalah: "those religious streams within Judaism," he explained, "which strive to arrive at a religious consciousness beyond intellectual apprehension, and which may be attained by man's delving into himself by means of contemplation, and the inner illumination which results from this contemplation."

This is almost too general a definition, given the complexities of the several generations and branches of Kabbalah (a word that means tradition, literally "what is received") in its luxuriant fecundity from the first millennium to its latest expression in the eighteenth century. The most influential of all these movements came to fruition in the town of Safed, in Galilee, in the sixteenth century, when an elite community of initiates gathered around Rabbi Isaac Luria and began to compose the astonishing works that comprise what is called the Lurianic Kabbalah. Not all the Lurianic ideas were new, but they expanded in an original direction under the pressure of one of the most catastrophic upheavals in Jewish history: the Inquisitorial persecutions of the Jews of Spain, and their expulsion after a golden age of high creativity. Here was yet another historic exile (the destruction of the Second Temple in the year 70, inaugurating the dispersion, was primal), and its thunderous effects had their mystical echo in a cataclysmic symbolism.

In the beginning—indeed, before the beginning—God's luminous essence filled the pleroma, the stuff of nothingness that was everywhere. Then God performed an act of *tsimtsum*, self-limitation, contracting in order to make room for Creation: "Without contraction there is no creation, as everything is God," Scholem writes. "Therefore, already in its earliest origins the creation is a kind of exile, in that it involves God removing Himself from the center of His essence to the secret places." But certain lights, or sparks, or brilliant emanations, of God trickled out nevertheless. These were the *sefiroth*, God's qualities or potentialities—the vital ten arteries, so to speak, of His Being. They can be listed as Primeval Will; Wisdom; Intuition; Grace; Judgment; Compassion; Eternity; Splendor; All Fructifying Forces; and last, the *Shekhinah*, "the hidden radiance of the totality of the hidden divine life which dwells in every created and existing being." These powerful divine lights flowed into the vessels that are the material of the created world; too fragile to contain such magnitudes, they broke apart, scattering the godly sparks. Some fell among the shards of the sundered vessels and were held captive, themselves damaged and given over to darkness. Because of this breakage, called *shevirah*, the ideal processes of Creation have been thwarted, and, ever since, nothing is in its right place; all is exile. In Lurianic Safed there arose, finally, the concept of *tikkun*, the reintegration of what has been fragmented, the correction of confusion, the return of harmony. In this way, the Kabbalists of Galilee, through a cosmological myth of exile and redemption, were able to map a people's shattered experience and adumbrate a vision of restoration.

It may have been in the early 1940s (there are no living witnesses, and no one of the current generation is certain just when) that Scholem was invited to New York to deliver a lecture on Kabbalah at the Jewish Theological Seminary. He was introduced by Saul Lieberman, a leading Talmudic eminence, and thereby an adherent of Jewish philosophical rationalism. "Nonsense is nonsense," said Professor Lieberman, "but the history of nonsense is scholarship." Whether Scholem responded to this now legendary maxim is not known. But the intensity, and the passion, of his scholarship intimate that he did not include visionary symbolism among the artifacts of nonsense.

§

In 1923, at twenty-six, Scholem set off for Palestine, as he had promised ten years before. He had completed his dissertation summa cum laude, and a post in a German university lay easily before him. Instead, he arrived in Jerusalem with six hundred volumes of Kabbalistic literature and no academic prospects. In Germany there were many universities; in Palestine there was none. But there were plenty of secondhand bookshops: Jerusalem, Scholem noted, "was saturated with old Hebrew books the way a sponge is saturated with water." By 1925 the Hebrew University of Jerusalem was inaugurated (it had been in the planning stage since 1913), and before long Scholem became its first professor of Jewish mysticism. And now began those torrents of innovative historical and literary scholarship, the voluminous output of a mind propelled by inquisitive desire, that quickly marked him as a twentieth-century luminary. He was not a man penetrating a field of learning; he was a field of learning penetrating the world. He wrote in a Hebrew that rivaled his native German in literary quality. He read Greek, Latin, Arabic, and Aramaic. His English was fluent and polished. *Major Trends in Jewish Mysticism*, lectures composed chiefly in English and first published in 1941, has become the standard introductory work: the dedication is "to the memory of Walter Benjamin, a friend of a lifetime." Scholem's magnum opus, *Sabbatai Sevi: The Mystical Messiah*, which appeared in English translation in 1973, is a consummate history of a seventeenth-century messiah figure who aroused, among the scattered Jewish masses, the hope of a return to Jerusalem; it is a book enormously suggestive of the origins of Christianity.

All this and more—lectures, teaching, travel to America, a second marriage, to Fanya Freud—Scholem accomplished during times of tumult and violence. In Germany, the crisis of postwar currency inflation was followed by the rise of Nazism, which harnessed and heightened a pervasive anti-Semitism. Scholem's brother Werner, against whom the earlier charge of treason had been ameliorated, was again arrested, both as a Communist and as a Jew; he was deported to Dachau, and was finally murdered in Buchenwald in 1940. In 1938, Scholem's widowed mother and his brothers Reinhold and Erich escaped to Australia. During these same years, Palestine was troubled by periodic Arab attacks on Jews, notably in 1920, 1921, 1929, 1936, and 1939. "For the past three months," Scholem wrote to Benjamin in August, 1936, "we in Jerusalem have been living under a state of siege. . . . There's a considerable amount of terrorism. . . . A few days ago a colleague of mine who teaches Arabic literature was murdered in his study while reading the Bible. . . . No one knows whether someone will toss a bomb his way or around the next corner." In June, 1939, he again told Benjamin, "We live in terror," and spoke of the "capitulation of the English"—the Mandate power—"in the face of violence." And in 1947 there was outright war when the surrounding Arab nations, rejecting the United Nations plan for the partition of Palestine, sent five invading armies to converge on the newborn Jewish state. Whole sections of Jerusalem were destroyed or overrun. Before Scholem's death, in 1982, he had lived through the terror incursions of 1956, the Six Day War of 1967, and the Yom Kippur attacks of 1973.

Scholem defined his Zionism as metaphysically and historically rooted rather than political. "I don't give a rap about the problem of the state," he said, and styled himself an anarchist. Nevertheless he joined colleagues at Hebrew University, in 1925, in the formation of Brit Shalom (Peace Covenant), a political group favoring a binational state, which was to include both Arabs and Jews on equal terms—but since few Arabs were attracted to the idea, and of these some were assassinated by other Arabs, it failed. He had once affirmed that by leaving Europe behind he was stepping out of world history in order to re-enter Jewish history; yet world history, it seemed, had an uncanny habit of following the Jews wherever they were. Scholem was compelled to endure intermittent chaos even as he probed into Kabbalistic theories of exile and redemption.

§

He also wrote letters. His father, toward whom he was never cordial, had died some months after Scholem's emigration. But he wrote often to his mother, who replied copiously, and now and then shipped him the familiar delicacies he requested—marzipan and sausage. He wrote to old friends still in Germany, to new friends in America; to his students; to Walter Benjamin, Theodor Adorno, Martin Buber, Hannah Arendt, George Lichtheim, George Steiner, Jürgen Habermas, Friedrich Dürrenmatt, Elias Canetti, Daniel Bell, Emil Fackenheim, Leo Strauss, Franz Rosenzweig (the author of *The Star of Redemption*, an ingenious and startling theological work that particularly drew Scholem's admiration), and scores of others. The letters comprise thousands of pages, unified by the force and striking crescendos of Scholem's uncompromising voice, and reverberating with the subterranean fires of a tumultuous intellect haunted by the enigmas of history, and by the accumulations of its own magisterial knowledge. In their unstinting energy they show a man exactly where he wanted to be, and conscious of exactly why.

His correspondents who were fleeing Germany were not so sure. Scholem repeatedly offered refuge to Benjamin, holding out the hope for a post at Hebrew University; Benjamin repeatedly vacillated, finally admitting to a procrastination "which is second nature to me when it comes to the most important situations in my life." To Scholem's exasperation, Benjamin was contemplating the feasibility of an island off Spain. "You could of course do your literary work here," Scholem countered. "Jerusalem offers more than Ibiza: first of all, there are people like us here; second, there are books. . . . But it seems to me doubtful that you'd feel comfortable in a land in which you took no direct part. . . . The only people who can survive all of the difficulties here are those who are fully devoted to this land and to Judaism." Benjamin, Scholem had come to recognize long before, had refused any such devotion; he had turned to Marxism. It was Hannah Arendt (then Hannah Stern), writing as a refugee in the south of France, who informed Scholem of Benjamin's suicide.

But for Scholem the most commanding chronicler of the growing Nazi harassment of Jews was Betty Scholem, his despairing mother. In a flood of anguished letters from Berlin (reminiscent of Victor Klemperer's diaries of gradual engulfment), she was recording a week-by-week tightening of the German noose. "I cannot digest what is happening," she wailed. "I'm completely speechless. I simply can't imagine that there are not 10,000 or

1,000 upright Christians who refuse to go along by raising their voice in protest." Her accounts of her futile trips to the offices of the Gestapo to appeal for information about the imprisoned Werner have the resonance of an atrocity foretold. In March, 1933, commenting on the Jewish lawyers, teachers, and physicians who were being barred from their professions, she wrote:

> It's a real stroke of luck that you're out of harm's way! Now, suddenly, I want to see everyone in Palestine! When I only think of the outcry heard among German Jews when Zionism began! Your father and grandfather Herman L. and the entire Central Verein beat themselves on the breast and said with absolute conviction, "We are Germans!" And now we're being told that we are not Germans after all!

Despite intervals of relative quiet, the Jewish population of Palestine was never entirely out of harm's way; but his mother's terrified response to the danger in Germany, years after his own prescient repudiations, left a bitter imprint on many of Scholem's later exchanges. In 1978 he declined to meet with Heidegger (as Buber had done) because Heidegger had been an unabashed Nazi. He was impatient with tendentious distortions of Jewish history. When an editor of the *New York Review of Books* asked him to review Arthur Koestler's *The Thirteenth Tribe: The Khazar Empire and Its Heritage*, Scholem's reply—"sensationalist humbug"—was scathing:

> Sigmund Freud told the Jews their religion was foisted upon them by an Egyptian, so that there was nothing for the Jews to be proud of. The Jews found it baseless but rather amusing. Some Gentiles loved it because it would teach those supercilious Jews a lesson. Arthur Koestler wants to give them the rest by telling them they were not even Jews and that

those damned Ashkenazim from Russia, Romania, and Hungary who had invented Zionism had not even the right to ask for Israel as their homeland—which their Khazaric forefathers had never seen. . . . There is nothing more to be said about Koestler's scholarship.

Some time earlier, in 1962, as part of a postwar, post-Holocaust effort toward official public remorse in Germany, Scholem was invited to contribute to a volume intended as homage to "the indestructible German-Jewish dialogue." He answered with a trenchant polemic:

> There is no question that Jews tried to enter into a dialogue with Germans, and from all possible perspectives and standpoints: now demanding, now pleading and imploring; now crawling on their hands and knees, now defiant; now with all possible compelling tones of dignity, now with a godforsaken lack of self-respect. . . . No one, not even someone who has long understood the hopelessness of this cry into the void, would belittle its passionate intensity and the notes of hope and sadness resonating from it. . . . No one responded to this cry. . . . The boundless ecstasy of Jewish enthusiasm never earned a reply in any tone that could count as a productive response to Jews as Jews—that is, a tone that would have addressed what the Jews had to give and not only what they had to give up. To whom, then, did the Jews speak in this famous German-Jewish dialogue? They spoke only to themselves. . . . In the final analysis, it's true that Germans now acknowledge there was an enormous amount of Jewish creativity. This does not change the fact that you can't have a dialogue with the dead.

This was not Scholem's most acerbic riposte, though it touched on one of the central passions of his historical thinking.

One year later, in 1963, Hannah Arendt published *Eichmann in Jerusalem: A Report on the Banality of Evil*, a polemical account of the trial of Adolf Eichmann, the high-ranking SS officer who had ordered the deportation of Jews to the death camps, and whom Israeli agents had captured in his Argentine hideout. Scholem's rebuttal ignited an intellectual conflagration that tore beyond the boundaries of their private exchange into a ferocious public quarrel. Arendt and Scholem had been warm correspondents, with admiration on both sides, for two decades. But as early as 1946 a fault line — not yet a crevasse — opened in their friendship. Arendt had sent Scholem "Zionism Revisited," an essay he dismissed as a "patently anti-Zionist, warmed-over version of Communist criticism" and "an act of political balderdash." He accused her of attacking the Jews of Palestine "for maintaining an otherworldly separation from the rest of mankind, but," he contended, "when these same Jews make an effort to fend for themselves, in a world whose evil you yourself never cease to emphasize, you react with a derision that itself stems from some otherworldly source." He set out his credo, both personal and political:

> I am a nationalist and am wholly unmoved by ostensibly "progressive" denunciations of a viewpoint that people repeatedly, even in my earliest youth, deemed obsolete. . . . I am a "sectarian" and have never been ashamed of expressing in print my conviction that sectarianism can offer us something decisive and positive. . . . I cannot blame the Jews if they ignore so-called progressive theories which no one else in the world has ever practiced. . . . The Arabs have not agreed to a single solution that includes Jewish immigration, whether it be federal, national, or binational. . . . [They] are primarily interested not in the morality of our political convictions but in whether or not we are here in Palestine at all.

> . . . I consider it abundantly obvious (and I hardly need emphasize this to you) that the political career of Zionism . . . has created a situation full of despair, doubt, and compromise —precisely because it takes place on earth, not on the moon. . . . The Zionist movement shares this dialectical experience of the Real (and all its catastrophic possibilities) with all other movements that have taken it upon themselves to change something in the real world.

He concluded by charging Arendt with cynical rhetoric aimed "against something that is for the Jewish people of life-and-death importance." Her view, he believed, was motivated by a fear of being classed as a reactionary, "one of the most depressing phenomena to be seen among clever Jews." He knew this, he said, from reading *Partisan Review*.

Vitriol ebbed and affection resumed. In the long run it was a friendship that could not be sustained, and with the appearance of *Eichmann in Jerusalem* Scholem's regard for Arendt dissolved; in old age he felt their dispute to have been "one of the most bitter controversies of my life." He disposed of "the banality of evil" as no better than a slogan: it contradicted and undermined the "radical evil" Arendt had testified to in *The Origins of Totalitarianism*, her earlier study. He argued against her merciless condemnation of the Jewish Councils whom the Germans had forced to run the ghettos: "I don't presume to judge. I wasn't there." He disagreed that the prosecution had failed to prove its case, even while he asserted his opposition to hanging Eichmann: "We should not make it easier for the Germans to confront the past . . . He now stands as a representative for everyone." He did not altogether quarrel with Arendt's criticism of the weaker elements of a people in extremis, but "to the degree that there really was weakness," he protested, "your emphasis is, so far as I can tell, completely one-sided and leaves the reader with a feeling of rage and fury." Rage and fury boiled up from a still deeper source:

> It is the heartless, downright *malicious* tone you employ in dealing with a topic that so profoundly concerns our life. There is something in the Jewish language that is completely indefinable, yet fully concrete — what Jews call *ahavath Israel*, or love for the Jewish people. With you, my dear Hannah, as with so many intellectuals coming from the German left, there is no trace of it. . . . In treating such a theme, isn't there a place for the humble German expression "tact of the heart"?

He ended with a familiar reproof: she was "filled with ressentiment for everything connected with Zionism"; her book did "nothing but mock Zionism — which is, I fear, the main point for you."

Arendt's response was unrelievedly hostile. She denied coming from the German left; she had come from German philosophy. She had no love for any nation or collective. As for her opinion of Zionism, the Jews no longer believed in God; they believed only in themselves. "In this sense," she told him, "I don't love the Jews."

§

Always deliberate in his language, Scholem initiated the term "the Catastrophe" for what is commonly known as the Holocaust. In his masterly scholarship the word hardly appears. But it is clear from his letters that the Catastrophe was one of the overriding preoccupations of his life, and a clandestine presence in his books. A goodly number of his correspondents were refugees; a few, among them his most treasured friend, were suicides. At the close of the war he roamed Europe, rescuing the surviving remnants of Judaica libraries and transporting them to Palestine. Together with Theodor Adorno, he succeeded in preserving another endangered archive: Walter Benjamin's papers, which he edited and guided into print. (Along the way he was delighted to learn that Benjamin was a direct descendant of Heinrich Heine.)

In the public arena—exemplified by the obsessions evident in his private writing—he pursued two prominent themes: the historical imperatives of modern Zionism; and German culpability and its subset, the delusions of German Jews in their unrequited love affair. As for the Germans themselves, "I can and would speak to individuals," but he withdrew from addressing the nation collectively. "We should allow time to do its work," he advised in 1952, noting that his visits to Germany on behalf of Jewish institutions "were among the most difficult and bitter I have ever experienced." These forays into biting polemics were never alien to Scholem; he had been oppositional since his teens. World-upheaval had buffeted his generation and cut down its most productive minds. "It's pointless to entertain any illusions: we have suffered a loss of blood," he wrote, "whose effects on the spirit and on scholarly achievement are simply unimaginable." Doubtless he had Benjamin in mind—but also the loss to intellectual history, especially in the form of advanced Jewish historiography. So it was left to Scholem to accomplish, single-handedly, the new historiography he envisioned, until the time when his students might take up his work and his legacy. In order to understand Kabbalah, he slyly told them, they must first read Kafka.

He formulated Kabbalah as myth—he was, after all, a modern. And as a modern transfixed by the unorthodox and the symbolic, he cast a seductive influence over realms far from his own demanding skills. Over the years the tincture of his mind colored the work of Harold Bloom, Jacques Derrida, Umberto Eco, Jorge Luis Borges, Patrick White, and every contemporary novelist lured by the figure of the golem (an artificial being whose occult genesis Scholem traced). These vagrant literary spores bemused him—"It's a free country," he once remarked—but he knew them to be distant from his powers and his mission. The uses of Kabbalah were not the enchantments of art or the ingenuities of criticism. For Scholem, Kabbalah was a fierce necessity, "the vengeance of myth against its conquerors." To classical Judaism, and its judgment of Kabbalah as heresy, he retorted:

> From the start this resurgence of the mythical conceptions in the thinking of the Jewish mystics provided a bond with certain impulses in the popular faith, fundamental impulses springing from the simple man's fear of life and death, to which Jewish philosophy had no satisfactory response. Jewish philosophy paid a heavy price for its disdain of the primitive levels of human life. It ignored the terrors from which myths are made. . . . Nothing so sharply distinguishes philosophers and Kabbalists as their attitude toward the problem of evil and the demonic.

For centuries, through persecutions and expulsions, forced conversions and torchings, to the abyss of the Catastrophe, Jews had suffered terror. Responding to these repeated crises, the mystical imagination had devised a cosmogony that incorporated Jewish historical experience. In Kabbalistic symbolism, with its tragic intuition that the world is broken, that all things are not in their proper places, that God too is in exile, Scholem saw both a confirmation of the long travail of Jewish dispersion, and its consolation: the hope of redemption. In short, he saw Zionism.

AND GOD SAW LITERATURE,
THAT IT WAS GOOD:
ROBERT ALTER'S VERSION

§ IN THE THIRD CENTURY B.C.E., Ptolemy Philadelphus, ruler of Alexandria, Egypt's most Hellenized and sophisticated city, determined that a Greek rendering of the Torah should be included in the Great Library of that famed metropolis. To that end, he sent lavish gifts to Eleazar, the high priest of the Temple in Jerusalem, who reciprocated by dispatching to Alexandria seventy-two sages, six from each of the twelve biblical tribes, to begin the work of translation. Ptolemy greeted the visitors with a banquet lasting seven days, after which they were taken to the island of Pharos. Here each man was shut up in his own cell, in strictest seclusion, each toiling separately over the Hebrew original, in order to perfect its transcription into the lingua franca of the age. Seventy days later, when the scribes emerged from their labors, it was revealed that the seventy-two individually calculated translations were identical, each to the other, varying not by a jot or a tittle. Hence the name Septuagint (meaning seventy), immemorially given to the miraculous Greek text: a book divine in its essence, and thereby divine in its production. When heaven has a hand in translation, it is bound to be immaculate. God, who is One, sees to the oneness—the indivisibility—of His word. Many scribes, but one authentic Voice.

Thus the legend. Yet stripped of the sacral, it encapsulates the most up-to-date thesis concerning the nature of the Hebrew Bible: that it can, after all, be read as a unity, indivisibly, like any literary work. The contemporary idea of reading the Bible as literature comes after two hundred years of strenuous philological sorting out, the purpose of which was to unravel what tradition had always held to be a tightly textured whole. Scholars, minutely excavating linguistic layers and Ugaritic cognates, pulled out disparate threads, and identified each according to its purported source and time. Instead of one Author, there were now several: the J writer, for whom God bore the name Yahweh (the German philologists' J Englished to our Y); the E writer, who invoked not Yahweh but Elohim; the P writer, a priest, or circle of priests, absorbed by the formalities of cult and rite; and finally D, the Deuteronomist. But even for the unravelers, who had zealously quartered the singularity of Transcendence, there was a unifier. This was the unknown Redactor, who, shrewdly concealing the seams, had spliced all four strands into canonical coherence. It was the Redactor whom the philologists sought to undermine. Below his work lay the multifaceted hidden truth.

For the ascendant Bible-as-literature movement—a movement, if it can sustain the term, confined mostly to university classes and those common readers drawn to Scripture for reasons other than pious belief—the Redactor returns not simply as an implied collator or pragmatic editor, but as a conscious literary mind, alert to every nuance of trope and type, whether verse or prose, from storytelling and the drama of character to national epic, from monotheistic grandeur to homely lentil stew. The Bible, then, can be read not for its authority (or not for its authority alone), but for its fastidious and deliberate art. But since Scriptural artfulness is also moral art, a potency of precept adheres to it nonetheless. The literary approach, writes Robert Alter, "directs attention to the moral, psychological, political, and spiritual realism of the biblical texts, which is a way of opening ourselves to something that deserves to be called their authority, whether we attribute that authority solely to the power of human imagination or to a transcendent source of illumination that kindled the imagination of the writers to express itself through these particular literary means."

The quotation is from Alter's 1991 volume, *The World of Biblical Literature*, which—along with *The Art of Biblical Narrative*, *The Art of Biblical Poetry*, and related earlier works—can, in retrospect, be seen as the arduously analytic preparation for an undertaking of such ambitiousness that to call it uncommon hardly suggests how very rare it really is. "Ethical monotheism," Alter sums up, "was delivered to the world not as a series of abstract principles but in cunningly wrought narratives, poetry, parables, and orations, in an intricate patterning of symbolic language and rhetoric that extends even to the genealogical tables and the laws." And in the most succinct summary of all, he cites the Talmudic view: "The Torah speaks in human language." Human language, yes, but who would dare to render Scripture single-handedly, all on one's own? In fact, in the entire history of biblical translation, there have been only three daredevil intellects, each inspired by profound belief, who have achieved one-man renditions: the Latin of Jerome, the German of Luther, and the English of William Tyndale. Tyndale, who was burned at the stake for his presumption in desiring the Bible to be accessible in the vernacular, is generally regarded as the forerunner of, or influence on, the King James Version—a work that is distinctly a committee enterprise. Though Jerome and Luther each had occasional rabbinic consultants, and Luther was advised also by Melancthon, a Reformist scholar, their translations stand as monuments to the power of individual rhetoric and intent. Luther in particular impressed on German as inexhaustible a linguistic force as the King James Version left on English. In English, notably, all significant biblical translation since Tyndale's sixteenth-century version, without exception, has been by committee. Until now.

That is why Robert Alter's intrepid Englishing of the Pentateuch, *The Five Books of Moses: A Translation with Commentary*, can be called historically astounding: with a gap of four hundred years, it comes directly after Tyndale. It will be seen to differ from standard American translations, whether it is the Anchor Bible, or the Revised English Bible, or the Jewish Publication Society's *Tanakh*, or any other significant collective project that may come to mind. Though not without manifold influences and appreciations (the medieval Ibn Ezra, for instance, or E. A. Speiser, a contemporary philological exegete), Alter aspires beyond erudition to the kind of sensibility a reader might bring to James or Proust. In this he scarcely means to reduce the hallowed stature of the biblical narratives, but the very opposite. Close attention to "the literary miracle of the stories," he points out in an introductory essay, will emphasize and intensify the rhetorical ingenuities by which "the chief personages are nevertheless imagined with remarkable integrity and complexity as individual characters . . . growing and changing through long stretches of life-experience." At the same time, he reminds us, the Hebrew Bible, unlike the novel of character and personal vicissitudes, "has been shaped to show forth God's overwhelming power in history, exerted against one of the great ancient kingdoms, and the forging of the nation through a spectacular chain of divine interventions that culminates in the spectacle of the revelation on the mountain of God's imperatives to Israel." So it is no wonder that previous translators, trembling before the transcendent majesty of the Hebrew text, have huddled together in protective consultative committees.

In one striking case, the consultants have not been present at the table. Everett Fox, relying on the work of the German-Jewish luminaries Martin Buber and Franz Rosenzweig, and adopting their approach of etymological mimesis—Hebrew roots cast as German roots—attempted a similar effect in English. Useful as a study guide and as a trot, it is not quite what we mean by translation, if translation is taken to be the avoidance of awkwardness. Fox's awkwardness is purposeful: "YHWH will pass over the entrance, / and will not give the bringer-of-ruin (leave) to come into your house to deal-the-blow" (Exodus 12:23). Helpful though this may be to the beginning student peering into the Hebrew, it is scarcely normative English.

Isaac Leeser, it ought to be noted, an eminent nineteenth-century German-born American rabbi, might have been able to claim the mantle of one-man translation (his was published in 1853) had he not clung so closely to the King James Version, faithful to its diction in general, and differing only in an occasional well-argued word: in Genesis, for instance, choosing "expansion" for "firmament."

So the opportunity for modern singularity, post-Tyndale, remains open to Alter. Yet what he has undertaken is not an act of hubris; it is a work of conviction. His conviction is twofold: first, the unextraordinary recognition that all translation is of its time, steeped in an impermanent idiom, ultimately to be superseded by the more familiar lingo of ongoing generations. The language of the King James Version is poetically enthralling and rightly revered, but our daily tongues no longer traffic in "walketh"s and "shalt"s (and we may be impatient with its deliberate, if only occasional, christological inaccuracies). It goes without saying that the foundational document of our civilization, as the Bible is often termed, needs to be understood in the language of its period; the drive toward the vernacular that defines Luther, Tyndale, and the King James Version is as urgent today as it was then, and perhaps more so now, when Scriptural references are alien to most undergraduates, and the majority of American synagogue congregations turn from the Hebrew text to the facing page, where the English translation resides.

If the necessity of contemporary usage were all that motivated Alter, he might have been content with the existing collective translations, despite their lack of stylistic force. But the second element drawing him to this mammoth work—he calls it "an experiment"—is the belief that it is precisely the discoveries of philological scholarship that have distanced readers through their preoccupation with lexical components and syntactical forms at the expense of insight, metaphor, tone, imagery, cadence, all spilling from the cornucopia of literary virtuosity. In short, the obstacle of philology's tin ear. Citing still another objection to contemporary modes of translation, Alter condemns "the heresy of explanation": as when, for example, the ubiquitous word "hand" (*yad* in Hebrew, a similarly strong monosyllable), a stoutly visual and flexible noun capable of multiple figurative effects, is "clarified" abstractly as "trust" or "care." ("And he left all that he had in Joseph's hands," Genesis 39:6.)

Alter also faults the common reliance on subordinate clauses to avoid parataxis, the distinctive biblical repetition of "and . . . and . . . and." Here we may recall E. M. Forster's witty formulation, in *Aspects of the Novel*, of plot as opposed to story: "'The king died and then the queen died' is a story. 'The king died, and then the queen died of grief' is a plot. The time-sequence is preserved, but the sense of causality overshadows it." Biblical narrative will have none of this. A typical series of statements connected by "and" complicates, it does not simplify, the reader's comprehension; implied causality haunts the chain of events through rhythmic repetition directed, in the way of a musical composition, at the interpretive ear. The Bible is all plot, all causality: its substance derives, after all, from the First Cause.

In arguing for the Bible's literary status, or standard, Alter maintains that "the language of biblical narrative in its own time was stylized, decorous, dignified," yet was never "a lofty style, and was certainly neither ornate nor euphemistic . . . a formal literary language but also, paradoxically, a plain-spoken one." And again: "A suitable English version should avoid at all costs the modern abomination of elegant synonymous variation, for the literary prose of the Bible turns everywhere on significant repetition, not variation." Finally, he insists that "the mesmerizing effect of these ancient stories will scarcely be conveyed if they are not rendered in a cadenced English prose that at least in some ways corresponds to the powerful cadences of Hebrew."

This, then, is the prescription: the task, the aim, the experiment Alter has set for himself. The heresy of explanation will be repudiated. The sound and sense of the original will be honored. Contemporary English will be employed, but not slavishly: "a limited degree of archaizing is entirely appropriate," he warns. And clearly Alter's vision includes the sweeping moral horizon that is the Bible's raison d'être. In addition, all this is to be accomplished while traversing vastly disparate regions of text and idea: the thematic and psychological Patriarchal Tales, the ritual instructions, the communal imperatives, and ultimately the pervasive assurance that the God of the Bible directs the course of history through an interdependent compact with humankind, and particularly with humankind's biblical stand-in, the nation of Israel.

Can Alter, working alone—sans colleagues, relying solely on his own instinct for the impress and idiom of two unrelated linguistic strands, as isolated in his toil as any of the fabled seventy-two—can he pull it off?

One might as well begin before the beginning, with pre-existence, before there was anything. Here are the first four verses of the profoundly familiar King James Version:

> In the beginning God created the heaven and the earth. And the earth was without form, and void; and darkness was upon the face of the deep. And the Spirit of God moved upon the face of the waters. And God said, Let there be light: and there was light. And God saw the light, that it was good; and God divided the light from the darkness.

And now Alter:

> When God began to create heaven and earth, and the earth then was welter and waste and darkness over the deep and God's breath hovering over the waters, God said, "Let there be light." And God saw the light, that it was good, and God divided the light from the darkness.

What can be discerned in these nearly identical passages? A syntactical disagreement over the first word, *b'reshit:* does the particle *b'* represent a prepositional phrase ("In the beginning") or a clause ("When God began")? Together with current scholarship, Alter votes for the clause. Where the King James Version introduces stops, breaking up the Hebrew into recognizable English sentences, Alter follows the uninterrupted flow of the original, subverting conventional English grammar, so that for a moment we are borne along with Joycean rapidity. For *ruah*, which can mean breath or wind or spirit, Alter chooses breath, the more physical—the more anthropomorphic—word. These in themselves are small and unsurprising innovations. What genuinely startles is the inspired coupling of "welter and waste," with its echoes of *Beowulf*ian alliteration perfectly conjoined, in sound and intent, with the Hebrew *tohu-vavohu*. A happening of this kind is one translator's own little miracle; no committee could hope to arrive at it.

But Alter's choice of "hovering," and especially the evocative footnote it triggers, may possibly lead to a muddling of one of his salient principles of translation. "*Hovering*," Alter notes, "the verb attached to God's breath-mind-spirit, elsewhere describes an eagle fluttering over its young and so might have a connotation of parturition or nurture as well as rapid back-and-forth movement." There is nothing to complain of in this valuable footnote; quite the opposite. It deepens, it enlarges, it leaps to associative imagery in the intuitive manner of poetry, and it is one of hundreds of equally illuminating glosses in a volume of more than a thousand pages. Nor are these copious amplifications all that Alter supplies for the sake of enriching the pristine text; besides the overall introductory essay, each of the Five Books has its own prefatory exposition.

Leviticus, for instance, lacking appealing human characters and a story, is often classed as an arid collection of rites and legalisms. But after reminding us that "small Jewish boys were introduced to the Torah not through the great story of creation and the absorbing tales of the patriarchs in Genesis but through Leviticus," Alter drills through this off-putting customary view to a distilling insight central to understanding the Hebrew Bible. "There is a single verb," he tells us, "that focuses the major themes of Leviticus—'divide' (Hebrew, *hivdil*). . . . What enables existence and provides a framework for the development of human nature, conceived in God's image, and of human civilization is a process of division and insulation—light from darkness, day from night, the upper waters from the lower waters, and dry land from the latter. That same process is repeatedly manifested in the ritual, sexual, and dietary laws of Leviticus." And he concludes:

"God's holiness, whatever else it may involve and however ultimately unfathomable the idea may be, implies an ontological division or chasm between the Creator and the created world, a concept that sets off biblical monotheism from the worldview of antecedent polytheisms." This is why tradition required little children to begin with Leviticus. Here Alter cites Rashi, a seminal exegete of the eleventh century: "Let the pure ones come and study the laws of purity."

In the light of Alter's declared opposition to "the heresy of explanation," what are we to infer from his vast and formidable critical engines? He has not chosen to publish his translation in the absence of embellishing footnotes and conceptual elaborations. He cleaves to interpretation, he does not eschew imaginative commentary, explication is zealously welcomed. Yet what is amply permitted outside the text is considered heresy within the text. This makes a muddle of sorts. Every translator knows, often despairingly, that accommodation must be allowed for, simply because the *ruah*—the spirit, indeed the respiratory apparatus—of each language is intrinsic and virtually unduplicable. Even when there are cognates (and there are none between Hebrew and English), the related words have their own distinctive character. In fact, *not* to accommodate can sometimes set off misdirection toward an implausible meaning.

Alter objects to the Revised English Bible's substitution of "offspring" for "seed" in God's promise to Abraham (Genesis 22:17): "I will greatly bless you and will greatly multiply your seed, as the stars in heaven and as the sand on the shore of the sea, and your seed shall take hold of its enemies' gate." (Both the Revised Standard Version and the Jewish Publication Society's *Tanakh* give "descendants.") If selecting the stronger noun were the only consideration, there could be no demurral. "Seed" yields a concrete image; it is of the earth; it includes, in the most literal way, the generative function (*semen*, Latin for seed); and it denotes the multiplicity of generations. "Offspring" is clumsy, even ugly, and is as far from God's dazzling stretches of stars and sand as this morning's newspaper is from William Blake. The difficulty is that the contemporary reader's linguistic expectations, long estranged from biblical idiom, is more attuned to the *New York Times* than to the "Songs of Innocence"; and if seed is not readily understood to mean progeny, who can make sense of "his seed shall take hold of his enemies' gate"? ("His enemies' gate" may be bewildering enough: to capture a "gate," the approach to a city, was to subjugate the city itself.) Despite Alter's reasoned liking for "a limited degree of archaization," his purpose in bringing ancient Hebrew into American English is, after all, to decrease the distance between Scripture and our quotidian lives. A modicum of textual accommodation—Alter's "heresy"—may cause poets and sticklers to sigh; but there are instances when a sigh must trump a muddle. And if Alter did not believe in enlightening twenty-first-century readers, he would have given us a translation as bare of the interpretive luxuriance of his scholia as a tree denuded of its innate verdancy.

On the other hand, Alter's determination to replicate the original as closely as possible, while it will surely satisfy the sticklers, will do more than that for the poets. The poets will rejoice. Alter's language ascends to a rare purity through a plainness that equals the plainness of the Hebrew. To achieve this, he has had to come to a clear decision about the nature of English, with its two sources, or etymological strands: the florid Latinate and the spare Germanic; or call it Dr. Johnson versus Lincoln. The voice of Alter's Hebrew-in-English is Lincoln's voice, whose words and meter resonate in American ears with biblical gravity and biblical promise. It is in this plainspeaking, quickly accessible Anglo-Saxon prose, simple monosyllable following simple monosyllable, that Alter lets us hear God's imperatives, pleas, hopes, and elations:

> . . . for the Lord shall turn back to exult over you for good as He exulted over your fathers, when you heed the voice of the Lord your God to keep His commands and his statutes written in this book of teaching, when you turn back to the Lord your God with all your heart and with all your being. For this command which I charge you today is not too wondrous nor is it distant. It is not in the heavens, to say, "Who will go up for us to the heavens and take it for us and let us hear it, that we may do it?" And it is not beyond the sea, to say, "Who will cross over for us beyond the sea and take it for us and let us hear it, that we may do it?" But the word is very close to you, in your mouth and in your heart, to do it. See, I have set before you today life and good and death and evil, that I charge you today to love the Lord your God, to go in His ways and to keep His commands and His statutes and laws. . . . Life and death I set before you, the blessing and the curse, and you shall choose life . . . (Deuteronomy 30:9–19)

Alter's gloss looks past this passage to the kind of world that surrounded it:

> The Deuteronomist, having given God's teaching a local place and a habitation in a text available to all, proceeds to reject the older mythological notion of the secrets or wisdom of the gods. It is the daring hero of the pagan epic who, unlike ordinary men, makes bold to climb the sky or cross the great sea to bring back the hidden treasures of the divine realm—as Gilgamesh crosses the sea in an effort to bring back immortality. This mythological and heroic era, the Deuteronomist

now proclaims, is at an end, for God's word, inscribed in a book, has become the intimate property of every person.

To which we might add, a book that is "not wondrous" requires no sacred mysteries, no sacred mediators, no sacred hierarchies. All the same, God's commands, statutes, and laws are not easy; they are grounded in self-restraint. Seven of the Ten Commandments begin with "Do not." And insofar as the overarching vision of monotheism encompasses ritual, it is as "a battle against the inchoate," Alter argues. "Authorized ritual is in all respects the exact opposite of ecstatic orgy (another departure in principle from the pagan world)."

Remarks like these — informational, historical, pedagogical — have a secularized socio-anthropological flavor so radically different in tone from the diction of the translation itself that we need to be reminded that Alter has crafted both. The text breathes out power and truth. The footnote is instructional. The one carries divine authority, the other carries . . . what? The authority of a teachers' manual, perhaps, the kind with the answers at the back of the book. But if the Bible in all the purity of its expression is genuinely and wholly intended to be read as *literature*, its prerogatives will descend to the level merely of prestige: the prestige of literature, which, as Alter has already defined it, derives its authority solely from "the power of human imagination." Literary prestige, though, tends to have a weak hold on authority, as the immemorial shufflings of the canon show us; otherwise the work of Virgil would still be as revered today as it was when the Latin spelling, Vergil, was deposed in favor of its Marian echo. The necessity of Virgil diminished when he came to be seen as Vergil the poet, not Virgil the prophet.

The necessity of the Bible, if it is to be seen solely as poetry and story, may flatten in the same way. All sacred books contain the wise or stirring pleasures of narrative: the Bhagavad-Gita tells stories, the Taoist scriptures of Chuang-Tsu tell stories, the Zoroastrian Zend-Avesta tells stories, the Koran tells stories, Confucius and Mencius tell stories, the Buddha tells stories; African and American Indian sacred tales abound. The earth is flooded with stories, hymns, and parables regarded as holy in their origins. The literary approach can deflate them all. The short story writer Flannery O'Connor, an intransigent believer, said of the Christian mysteries that if they were not true, "then the hell with them." A skilled teller of tales, she insisted on a distinction between imagination of the kind she herself could wield and what she took to be divine revelation. And it may be that if all the world's scriptures had long ago been flattened into literature, and packed side by side, despite their dissimilarities and divergences, into a single bookshelf—much as *Madame Bovary*, say, can stand in civil proximity to *Crime and Punishment*, and Joyce cheek by jowl with Proust—all our habitations and histories might have been far more pacific. Novels and stories do not war with one another; neither, *pace* Harold Bloom, do they always engage in supersessionism (at least not of the jihadist variety).

But stories, though they influence and enlarge us, do not deliver Commandments. The Bible cannot be pumped up from literary prestige to divine prerogative through arguing from the power of human imagination, even when that power is "kindled" by positing measureless structures of transcendent dominion. What, then, are unbelieving readers of the Five Books left with? Unless they happen to be moral philosophers who will deduce law and right conduct from reason, it is stories they are left with, and—for nonphilosophers—isn't that enough? On their face, the Patriarchal Tales, like all literature that endures, touch on everything recognizable in ordinary human life: crises between parents and children, between siblings, between husbands and wives;

hunger and migration, jealousy and reconciliation, sudden ascent and sudden subjugation, great love and great hatred. Universally felt, they are family annals in a family album. The Joseph narrative is doubtless the most moving story of all: here stands Joseph, Pharaoh's mighty viceroy, interrogating the humbly petitioning brothers who in the past flung him into a pit and sold him to traders on their way to Egypt. Catching sight of Benjamin, the tender younger son of Rachel, their mother, "Joseph hurried out, for his feelings for his brother overwhelmed him and he wanted to weep, and he went into the chamber and wept there. And he bathed his face and came out and held himself in check and said, 'Serve bread.'"

In this enclosed fraternal scene, God is not needed, and seems not to be present. So far, the drama of Joseph appears to resemble the stories we call literature; and yet it does not, because Joseph will not permit God to be exiled out of his world. When, bowing before Pharaoh's deputy, the brothers plead for forgiveness, Joseph is again swept into weeping, and invokes not only God, but God's design: "And Joseph said, 'Fear not, for am I instead of God? While you meant evil for me, God meant it for good.'" And further: "Do not be pained and do not be incensed with yourselves that you sold me down here, because for sustenance God has sent me before you . . . to make you a remnant on earth and to preserve life, for you to be a great surviving group. And so, it is not you who sent me here but God." A few verses on, Joseph dies, at one hundred and ten, and is embalmed according to Egyptian custom. And now, portentously, the Book of Genesis ends: "He was put in a coffin in Egypt."

That coffin signifies more than a human story. It is God's story: Egypt will become a coffin for the Hebrews until God redeems them. God in the Hebrew Bible is Causality, and Causality, unlike Joseph or Benjamin, cannot be a character in a tale—an assertion that has been broadly contradicted, or at least qualified, in formulations by both Harold Bloom and Jack Miles. In his winning and ingenious *God: A Biography*, Miles is moved to ask, "How did all this feel to God?" and sets out to see Him as a "character who 'comes to life' in a work of literary art." Miles's God has an indelible, even a familiar, human personality, not unlike the mercurial protagonist of an epic, or an opera, or a labyrinth of motives by Henry James. And while it may be possible to transmute aspects of Scripture into literature by means of the fictive imagination—certainly Thomas Mann succeeded in turning the Joseph chronicle into a massive and masterly novel—finally Scripture itself rebels against it. Mann's fiction can claim no greater authority than writerly genius.

Just here is the nub and the rub of it: if the God of the Bible is not "real," then—in creative-writing-course argot—the Bible's stories won't and don't *work*. For the faithless skeptic or rationalist confronting Scripture (a category of modernity that includes, I suppose, most of us), there is nothing more robust to lean on than suspension of disbelief, the selfsame device one brings to Jane Austen. Mr. Darcy and Mr. Knightly, salvational creations both, are not real; we believe in them anyway. Causality deserves better. Causality escapes the mere "comes to life" of character.

It is the directness and consummate clarity of Alter's rendering that forces this conclusion. The translator's richly developed notes and reflections are informed by scholarship, wit, and intuition; without the intrusions of didacticism, they educate. But the antique words, on their own power, and even in a latter-day language, draw us elsewhere, to that indeterminate place where God is not a literary premise but a persuasive certainty—whether or not we are willing to go there.

An (Unfortunate) Interview
with Henry James

§ THE INTERVIEW TOOK PLACE at Lamb House, Rye, Sussex — rather, its precise duplicate in the Other World. The house, red brick with numerous mullioned windows, fronts the street. One approaches it along the curve of a narrow flagstoned path. Four shallow steps lead up to a white door overhung by a cornice. The modest brass knocker is tapped, and a young man responds. He is Burgess Noakes, James's valet.

JAMES (*within*): Noakes? Is it our appointed visitor?

NOAKES: Yes, sir. It's the American lady from that magazine.

JAMES (*coming forward with a certain fussy anxiety*): A lady? I was rather expecting a gentleman. Forgive me, dear madam, do come in. — Noakes, the tea things, if you please. — Ah, my most admirable typewriter is just departing. Quite a morning's toil, Miss Bosanquet, was it not? We are getting on, we are getting on!

Miss Theodora Bosanquet, James's typist (writer's cramp has in recent years forced him to dictate), emerges from a room behind, pinning on her hat. She neatly rounds James's bicycle, precariously lodged against an umbrella stand in the central hall. She nods, smiles tiredly, and makes her way out with practiced efficiency.

JAMES (*seating himself before a finely tiled fireplace, and motioning for the visitor to join him there*): I must again beg your pardon. I discover myself increasingly perplexed by the ever-accelerating extrusions of advanced women —

INTERVIEWER (*interrupting*): You don't like us. You were opinionated enough about all that in *The Bostonians.*

JAMES (*taken aback by this feminist brashness, and glad to have Noakes deflect it with the arrival of a tray holding teacups and a variety of jellied pastries*): Thank you, Noakes. The advent of cakes, the temptation to the sweet tooth, how it brings to the fore one's recent torments at the dentist's! One must perforce disclose one's most private crannies to this oral Torquemada — which I take to be the unhappy emblem of an age of interlocutory exposure. The ladies seem to swim in it! Especially the American ladies.

INTERVIEWER: I suppose that's what you were getting at in your portrait of Henrietta Stackpole, the peppy American journalist in *The Portrait of a Lady.*

JAMES: May I say, *mutatis mutandis*, that *she* might have been getting at me! In point of fact, dear madam, I have in mind rather my unfortunate engagement with your predecessor, an American lady journalist representing the *New York Herald*, with whom I sat, as it were, for an interview during my American journey in 1904, my maiden voyage, so to speak, into a venture of this kind. This lady's forwardness, her hagiographical incessancy, was, in fine, redoubtable. She hastened to remark upon how I had so far, and so long, escaped the ministrations of uncanny inquirers such as herself, and undertook to portray my shrinking from her certainties as a species of diffident bewilderment. She declaimed it her right, as a free citizen of my native land, to put to me all manner of intimacies. I warned her, as I now warn you, madam, that one's craft, one's art, is in one's expression, not one's person. After you have heard Adelina Patti sing, why should you care to hear the small private voice of the woman?

INTERVIEWER: I gather that you intend to inhibit my line of questioning.

JAMES: Madam, I do not inhibit. I merely decline to exhibit.

INTERVIEWER: Is that why you've had the habit of burning things? When your ailing sister Alice died, her companion, Katharine Loring, had copies of Alice's diary printed up especially for you and your brother William. You burned your copy.

JAMES: Ah, the mask and armour of her fortitude, poor invalid!—and with such ironic amusement and interest in the presentation of it all. It would not, could not, do. My fraternally intimated morsels of London gossip, for the simple change and relief and diversion of it, came ultimately, and distressingly, to animate her pen. The wit of those lucubrations loomed, may I say, as a vulgar peril. So many names, personalities, hearsays, through *me!* I hardly wished to be seen as privately depreciating those to whom I was publicly civil.

INTERVIEWER: Yet in 1909 you might have been seen as doing exactly that. You made a bonfire in your garden of the thousands of letters sent you by your devoted correspondents, many of them your distinguished friends. And six years later, you threw still more papers into the fire: it took you a week to get the job done. Will you agree that you've been singularly merciless to your biographers?

JAMES: Put it that the forewarned victim subverts the future's cunning. I have been easier in my mind ever since, and my

little conflagrations scarcely appear to have impeded poster-
ity's massive interventions.

INTERVIEWER: Well, true, they haven't stopped us from spec-
ulating that you're gay and always have been.

JAMES: Indeed, there has been a frequency of jolly corners . . .
delightful hours with Turgenev in Paris . . . the soliloquizing
intimacy of one's London hearth in winter, or the socially
convenient pleasures of the ever so felicitous Reform Club
. . . going in to dinner with a gracious lady on one's arm in
some grand country house . . . all rewardingly gay at times,
to be sure; but neither have I been spared sojourns upon the
bench of desolation. Despair, I own, dogged me in particular
in the year 1895, when at the opening of my play, *Guy
Domville*—

INTERVIEWER (*breaking in hurriedly*): I mean you've loved
men.

JAMES: And so I have. To choose but one, my fondness for the
dear Jonathan Sturges, that crippled little demon, resonates
unchecked for me even now. How I embraced the precious
months he came to stay at Lamb House, with his mordant
tongue and bright eyes, full of unprejudiced talk and intelligence. Body-blighted Brother Jonathan! Yet he made his way
in London in wondrous fashion.

INTERVIEWER: I'm afraid we're not entirely on the same
page.

JAMES: The same page? Would that be an Americanism? With
all your foreign influx, we shall not know our English tongue
for the sacred purity it once resplendently gave out. A young
American cousin, on a visit here, persisted in pronouncing
"jewel" as "jool," "vowel" as "vowl," and was driven at last to
deem my corrections cruel. "'*Cru-el*,' Rosina, not '*crool*,'" I

necessarily admonished. The young ladies of Bryn Mawr College, in the vicinity of Philadelphia, when I lectured there in 1905, had similar American afflictions. They would articulate the reticent "r" in words such as *motherrrr, fatherrrr, millerrrr*—

INTERVIEWER: I admit to that "r" myself. But to come back to your, um, fondness for men. One of your more reckless biographers believes that in the spring of 1865, in your own shuttered bedroom in Cambridge—that's Cambridge, Massachusetts—you had your earliest experience, your *initiation première*, as you yourself called it in your journal.

JAMES: Ah, the epoch-making weeks of that memorable spring! The bliss of *l'initiation première*, the divine, the unique! It was in that very March that my first published story appeared in the *Atlantic Monthly*.

INTERVIEWER: We're definitely not on the same page. He claims that this *initiation première* of yours was in the arms of the young Oliver Wendell Holmes, Junior, the future chief justice of the United States Supreme Court. He says that you slept with Holmes. Carnally.

JAMES (*recoiling, and pressing his fingers to his temples, as if a familiar migraine is coming on*): My dear lady—

INTERVIEWER (*digging into her tote bag and pulling out a thick biographical volume*): And what about Hugh Walpole? No one burned *your* letters, after all. Here's what you wrote to your "dear, dear Hugh": "See therefore, how we're at one, and believe in the comfort I take in you. It goes very deep— deep, deep, deep: so infinitely do you touch and move me, dear Hugh." Such obvious ardor! What do you say to it?

JAMES: I say I deeply, deeply, infinitely favour the universalization of epistolary arson. The twaddle of mere graciousness has perhaps too often Niagara'd from the extravagances of my inkpot.

INTERVIEWER: And how about your "exquisite relation" with Jocelyn Persse? A good-looking Anglo-Irishman, the nephew of Lady Gregory, thirty when you met him, you were sixty. Now it was "my dear, dear Jocelyn." You went so far as to ask for his photo to moon over. And then there was Hendrik Andersen, that big handsome blond Norwegian sculptor—"I have *missed* you," you confided, "out of all proportion to the three meagre little days that we had together. I hold you close, I feel, my dear boy, my arms around you, I draw you close, I hold you long." So why shouldn't the homoerotic question come up?

JAMES (*reddening*): Andersen's sculptures, those monstrously huge swollen ugly things. Let us pass over this unseemly subject.

INTERVIEWER: Here in the twenty-first century we pass over nothing, we let it all hang out. You mentioned earlier your despondency over your theatrical failure.

JAMES: Madam, you hurl me from unseemliness to unseemliness! The *sacro terrore* of it all! My charmingly contemplated eloquences were vigorously upon the boards when out of nervousness I slipped out to sample a neighboring drama— *An Ideal Husband*, Oscar Wilde's juvenile folly, flailing its silly jocularity. When I returned to the St. James, the last act was just finishing—there were cries of "Author, author"—and then the hoots and jeers and catcalls of the roughs began— roars—a cage of beasts at some infernal zoo—

INTERVIEWER: You fell into a long depression after that. One of the many in your life, despite brilliant friendships, fame, the richness of travel, Paris, Rome, Florence, Venice, family visits to America—

JAMES: Never say you know the last word about any human heart.

INTERVIEWER: But George Bernard Shaw was in the audience as a reviewer that night, and he praised and championed you. You've had scores of champions and admirers — Edith Wharton, for one.

JAMES: The Firebird! Her motoring habits and intentions, so potent and explicit, bent on catching me up in her irresistible talons, the whir and wind of those great pinions cold on my foredoomed brow! Oh, one's opulent friends — they cost the eyes out of one's head. Edith, always able and interesting, yet insistent and unpredictable. Her powers of devastation were ineffable.

INTERVIEWER: She came with her car and her chauffeur and took you away from your work. But she also facilitated it. There was that scheme she cooked up, getting your mutual publisher to give you a portion of her bestseller royalties — eight thousand dollars — while pretending they were your earnings. It was arranged so shrewdly that you swallowed it whole. And then she took up a collection for your seventieth birthday —

JAMES: A more reckless and indiscreet undertaking, with no ghost of a preliminary leave asked, no hint of a sounding taken — I am still rubbing my eyes for incredulity. I undertook instant prohibitive action. It was shame heaped on shame, following as it did on the failure of my jubilant yet woebegone New York Edition, for which I had had such vain hopes, the hopes, alas, of my vanity — my labors uniformly collected, judiciously introduced by the author, and improved upon according to the author's maturer lights. I have been remarkably unwanted and unread.

INTERVIEWER: Not lately. They make films of your stories

and novels. They make novels of your life. You're an indus-
try in the graduate schools. But isn't there something of this
frustration in "The Next Time," your tragicomical short
story about a literary genius who hopes to turn himself into a
popular hack so as to sell, to be read?

JAMES (*gloomily*): With each new striving he can draw out only
what lies in him to do—another masterwork doomed to obscurity. Poor fellow, he falls short of falling short!

INTERVIEWER: Which is more or less what happened to you
when you were writing Paris letters for the *New York Tribune*
at twenty dollars apiece. It ended with your getting sacked
for being too good. Your brother saw it coming—he'd
warned you not to lose hold of the pulse of the American
public. You were over their heads.

JAMES (*with some bitterness*): William instructed me, in point of
fact, and not for the first time, to pander. I gave it my best,
which is to say my worst. It was the poorest I could do, especially for the money!—Madam, is there to be more of this
extraordinary discourse?

INTERVIEWER: Well, I did want to ask about the women in
your life. Your tubercular young cousin, Minny Temple, for
instance, who inspired your heroines Daisy Miller and Isabel
Archer and Milly Theale . . . she pleaded with you to let her
join you in Rome, a city she longed to see, hoping the
warmer climate would cure her—

JAMES: The sublime, the generous, the always vivid Minny!
Yet in the pursuit of my then burgeoning art, I could not
possibly have taken on the care of a dying young woman.

INTERVIEWER: And what of your friendship with Constance
Fenimore Woolson? A novelist of sensibility herself, who
hung on your every word . . . you stashed her away, you kept

your frequent visits to her a great secret from your London circle—

JAMES: I had a dread of being, shall we say, "linked" with Miss Woolson. I feared the public charge of an "attachment." But she was deranged, poor lady. She was not, she was never, wholly sane.

INTERVIEWER: You decided this only after she jumped out of a window in Venice and killed herself. Until then you regarded her, in your own words, as "a deep resource." She put aside her own work for the sake of yours. You exploited her.

James is silent. The fire's flicker darts across the vast bald dome of his Roman head. Then, with a faint groan—he is notably corpulent—he rises from his armchair.

JAMES (*calling out*): Noakes, will you be good enough to escort our visitor to the door?—Ah, my dear lady, let us bring this fruitless exchange to the termination it has long merited. I observe with regret that you possess the modern manner—you proceed rather in the spirit of an assizes, you place me in the dock! You scrutinize without scruples. You pry into the dignified celibacy of a contented bachelorhood. Heartlessly you charge on, seizing upon one's humiliations, one's defeats —Mount Ossa on Mount Pelion! You come, in fine, not to praise Caesar, but to bury him. Put it then, madam, that you and I are not, cannot, shall never be, on the same page!

NOAKES (*considerately*): Mind the Master's bicycle don't strike you in the shins, ma'am. Miss Bosanquet, hers was black-and-blue, but she's got used to it, and goes round.

The interviewer picks up her tote bag (unbeknownst to James, a tape recorder is hidden in it), and also one of the jellied pastries, and wordlessly departs.